What the critics have said about *Tips and tactics for surviving pregnancy and the first twelve months ...*

'No one wants to read about nappies and teething, dude!'
(Author's best mate — single, non-parent)

'... Although, if I'm seen reading it at a café, chicks might think I'm sensitive and caring!'
(Author's best mate — single, non-parent, idiot)

'... Oh, no, that's no good. They might think I'm married!'
(Author's best mate — single, non-parent, idiot, loser)

'I always knew you would be a literary genius!'
(What author's mother should have said)

'That's not how you spell mastitis!'
(What author's mother really said)

BLOKES AND BABIES

Tips and tactics for surviving pregnancy and the first twelve months

Brad Storey

Lothian BOOKS

For Jodi-anne.
More than the moon and the sun and the stars.

Thomas C. Lothian Pty Ltd
132 Albert Road, South Melbourne, Victoria 3205
www.lothian.com.au

First published 2005

National Library of Australia
Cataloguing-in-Publication data:
Storey, Brad
Blokes and babies: tips and tactics for surviving pregnancy and the first twelve months
ISBN 0 7344 0817 X.
1. Father and infant. 2. Fatherhood. 3. Pregnancy. I. Title
306.8742

Cover and text design by Christa Moffitt
Cover photograph by Shannon Morris
Typesetting by John van Loon
Printed in Australia by Griffin Press

WARNING

This book contains 'secret men's business'.

It is addressed solely to men — in the knowledge that they will not disclose the content to anyone of female persuasion, nor allow a woman to peruse its pages.

This is a commitment you must make now before reading any further. It is a bond of brotherhood (or is that fatherhood?) that I am confident will not be broken.

FOREWORD

by Jonathan Coleman

Just three little words ... So powerful, thrilling and life changing. And just three little words!

No, no, no. Not *those* three little words. Not 'I love you'! What's the big deal about those three words? You can love a dog. You can love a car. You can loooooove pineapple daiquiris! No, 'I love you' is just too common. Love comes, love goes; sometimes you can be in love and not even know it. As powerful phrases go, 'I love you' is just too run-of-the-mill.

No, if you want three little words that can literally change your life — words that can take your breath away and slam you flat on your butt — then these three are the ones. These three little words have the same effect on men across the universe, no matter their age, race, religion or creed ... these three little words change the direction of your life forever. They are:

'Darling, I'm pregnant!'

Oh yeah! Now that's powerful — that's what I call life changing. That's what I call 'heavy' — even for a guy like me!

That's why *Blokes and Babies: Tips and tactics for surviving pregnancy and the first twelve months* is a must-read for every red-blooded man. It uncovers secrets hidden away from men throughout the millennia. And let's face it, when it comes to those three little words, we need all the help we can get.

It's my fervent hope that the information in this book will go some small way to preparing you for the life-transforming experience that is fatherhood. It may even prepare you for your first full nappy experience! ... Well maybe, but forewarned is definitely forearmed my friend.

So, good luck fella ... you're going to need it as much as you'll need this book!

Jono Coleman

Husband of long-suffering Margot and fatherhood survivor of Oscar and Emily.

CONTENTS

Acknowledgements

This book came about due to a forced retrenchment three weeks after the birth of my child. While there was a general wailing and gnashing of teeth, railing at a cold, heartless world, I found from the ashes of my de-railed career one of the most precious gifts I've ever received. I was given the gift of time with my wife and new baby, something few men ever get to fully experience.

From observing the usual, regular, mundane and everyday of life with a baby I soon began to see the absurd and downright weird. In fact I was probably enjoying the experience too much. I decided it really was time to return to the 9 to 5 when I overheard my wife one day telling a friend that our child 'has two mummys'!

I'd like to thank Averill Chase for her faith in taking on this project, Amy Thomas for guiding the production, Stephen Grimwade who knocked my garbled sentences into a form other people could understand and Matt Golding for his wonderful and numerous cartoons: *Blokes and Babies* wouldn't be the same without them.

Particular thanks to Brian Cook for his guidance and belief.

Most importantly thank you to my beautiful wife Jodi-anne* for her constant encouragement, love and support.

*Any similarity between my wife and the cranky, hormonal, weeping, scary, demanding women discussed in the following pages is purely coincidental.

MAAAAAATTE
maaaaaaate
GOLDING

INTRODUCTION

Hi. How are you doing? OK? Take a deep breath — try to relax a little. Remember, you've found a friend. I'm on your side. We'll try to get through this thing together. Feeling a little nauseous? That's all right — you've come to the right book.

What you'll read in the following pages won't make your 'condition' go away but will assist you in dealing with it, particularly in the early stages. By 'early stages' I mean years because you now have a lifelong affliction.

Whoa! Whoa there big fella! Stay calm! Breathe. Here, let me share a little story with you ... My friend Paul works in the media — radio to be specific. As you would expect with a person who labours with language, he is witty, intelligent and eloquent. He is, in fact, a 'paid communicator'. But it must be told here that the mere thought of impending fatherhood was enough to reduce this media professional to a gibbering idiot. (Truth be known — most people on radio are gibbering idiots!) See if this statement sounds familiar to you:

'Emma and I are ... well ... We've decided to ... ahhh ... Ummmm ... We're thinking about ... kind of ... trying to ... like maybe ... sort of ... have a baby ... type of ... errr? ... Thingy! ... You know?'

Oh, yeah, I know all right!

For Paul and any other male in this predicament, that means the sex *sort of thingy* is now *au naturel*. Talk about performance anxiety! And so it is for the

unprepared *pre-parents*, like Paul, about to embark upon the journey to parenthood that I have put down some of the things I wish I had been told.

You see, I was once just like you. I too went tremblingly in search of wisdom only to be faced with row upon row of book covers with smiling mothers and chubby babies. Titles like:

You and Your Womb

Triumphant Trimesters — a 230 day guide to gestation

Motherhood in the Third Millennium (sounds like 1960s sci-fi!)

An Intimate ... (Quite frankly, anything with 'intimate' in the title stopped me dead in my tracks. That word reeks of feminine 'mystique' and things to do with being a woman that I'm sure are none of my business.)

What was there for the rest of us? The guys! The fellas! The blokes! We don't need to know about wombs and amniotic fluid! We need advice about important things — advice that's rational and useful, that'll answer questions like, 'When the kid's born, how long till I can have sex again?'

Well, I couldn't find anything, so I felt it to be nothing short of my moral duty to assist the 50 per cent of the human population that had been ignored and dismissed! (Yeah, OK, 'moral duty' and the hope that the royalties from book sales would quickly net me a longed-for luxury yacht anchored in sparkling Mediterranean waters.)

So now you know what's in it for me — what's in this book for you? The following pages will show you that there are things to do with mothers and babies that can be anticipated, planned and prepared for. You will also come to realise there are *other* things to do with mothers and babies that are absurd, unreasonable and make no sense whatsoever; these you must offer to the universe as unalterable.

'Nothing new there,' I hear you say but wait up … Once a woman is pregnant she is no longer the usual garden variety of illogical, weeping, shopaholic female you're used to. Rather she is a new kind of female. One who is, in fact, 'super charged' with hormonal imbalance.

Within these pages you will discover that, like so much in the irrational world of women and their hormones, surviving this new phase of your life requires an adjustment in *perspective* (and possibly the assistance of some mild sedation). Within these pages you will be taught skills to assist in finding the meditative peace that stops your rational, logical male brain from asphyxiating.

Of course, to begin with, you may find advice

such as: 'Do what she tells you', 'Do as she says' and 'For the love of God, don't fight with her or she'll suck your eyeballs out', a little weak. But I'm confident as you progress through these pages, as more and more of the unimagined horrors are revealed, you'll come to accept the simple wisdom.

Most importantly, I hope this book will help you to enjoy the benefits of being a sensitive, caring dad openly able to enjoy your new baby (and there is nothing better), while at the same time maintaining your healthy male exterior, a façade of rugged blokiness to show the outside world, your buddies and business colleagues.

JUST TRYING TO GIVE YOU SUPPORT HONEY!
IT'S OK I GUESS, BUT YOU'RE A BIT LUMPY!

Chapter 1

Hormones — She's Got 'Em

So, you've *heard* about 'hormones' but what do you *really* need to know? Well, basically fella, she's got 'em and you don't, so get used to it!

I don't care whether you're a gynaecologist majoring in paediatrics with a masters degree in child psychology — you will never be able to claim that you are closer to your baby than its mother. You see, once pregnant, a woman *knows* and she knows all sorts of stuff.

She knows by instinct, she knows intuitively and she knows that all the books and magazines and classes and videos and secondhand advice from grandparents and relatives and medical experts is just so much puffery. She has the hormones ... and you don't, and that's all *you* need to know.

You have now officially reached the status of 'drone' and you must quickly assume the position of kowtowing novice in just about anything to do with child rearing. (Well, until your child reaches some useful stage of development when you can sit down and discuss important things together; serious, rational and useful things like sport and cars ... and how to get rid of a hangover.)

In fact, as a father-to-be, you get kind of used to this feeling of *helplessness* — actually it's more knowinglessness — a kind of constant uneasy feeling of being a paper boat sailing down a rain-swollen gutter. You see, not just your wife or partner but pretty much everyone around you knows more about babies than you do. Grandparents, doctors, your boss, even little girls that live down the road. Everyone seems to know about babies except you — 'big dumb Daddy'!

Don't get me wrong. When it comes to your pregnant partner or wife, it's not that you *can't* be right; it's just that she can *never* be wrong! It doesn't matter how much you know, how much you think you know, or how much you empathise or try to empathise. Your role is not to question or debate. Your role is to 'support'.

'Support' is now what you do. That's about as much involvement as your position of drone extends to.

'Support' however can be a hell of a lot more difficult than it sounds because it involves second-guessing your partner ... and blokes know how dangerous that can be!

You see, along with her *all knowing* hormones, comes the added ability to effortlessly make you feel as totally useless as possible. This is because, despite your best efforts and intentions, you will never give *enough* support or the *correct* support. This is because no one knows for sure, at any given moment, exactly what kind of support you're supposed to give. It is totally up to the individual. (Not you ... her!) It may be a back rub, it may be an ice-cream, it may be a warm bath, it may be soothing music ... Or it may be packing your bags, moving interstate and keeping out of her way for a few months.

'Support' means something different to every woman every moment of the day, and this is one of life's challenges for we drones. Exactly what she wants and when she wants it is entirely up to her. And if you don't figure out what it is she wants and deliver it to her the moment she decides she wants it (or at least physically injure yourself in the attempt), then you are likely to be accused of being 'insensitive', 'cold', 'distant', 'thoughtless', 'unbearable', 'selfish', 'manipulative', 'shallow', 'heartless', 'uncaring' or 'not interested in the baby'. Worst of all you could be told, 'You're just not supportive!'

Of course, this is a total no-win situation for the drone. Your partner doesn't know what she wants until she decides she wants it, by which time it's too late for you to provide it ... but that's not the point! If you were any kind of man you'd *know* what she wants just like she *knows* what's going on with the baby. And guess what? It all makes perfectly rational sense to her. She has the hormones and you don't, so what would you *know* anyway?!

All this is made abundantly clear to you by most of the professionals you meet: you are the drone and for the most part your job is already done ... *and* it wasn't anything special anyway. Just about every midwife I met, not to mention nurses, counsellors, obstetricians and even the doctor's secretary, all seemed to look down on me in the same condescending way. It's kind of like you're a dog who's dug up something distasteful from the garden, or waggled on home with a new mate.

> Aren't we proud of ourself, hmmmm? Managed to pass on our genetic material have we? Managed to figure that bit out? And did we have a good time doing it fella? Did we? I'll bet we did! We're just soooo clever aren't we? Just about the smartest little man there's ever been.

> So why don't we just curl up there in the corner with a magazine and be quiet ... We women will do the rest. Yes! ... *we* will call *if* we need you. Now be a good boy, just try to keep out of our way and be quiet. No! Very nice of you to ask but we don't need any assistance right now. *We* are the nurturers. This is our domain and the world would be a whole lot nicer place if it wasn't for the likes of ... *you.*

It's the kind of experience that scares men into believing if women held the seats of power there would be no more war. Everyone would meet to *share* their feelings, have a cry, eat a bucket of ice-cream, then go away and — instead of shooting each other — have a bloody good bitch instead!

'That President of Bulgaria, who does she think she is? And what was she thinking wearing *that* to a summit meeting? As for the Prime Minister of India, she really needs to get out more.'

It doesn't change too much after the bundle of joy arrives either. In fact, it becomes a whole lot more intense. Whenever there are a number of answers to a question or scenario concerning the baby, you will always choose the wrong one. (This is because she has the hormones and you don't.) Some examples:

'Do you think he's hungry?'

'No, he's teething.'

'Is he tired?'

'No, he needs changing!'

'Should I give him a drink?'

'No, he wants to play with the ball!'

'What about a little bit of chicken? I think he'd like it.'

'What are you — a complete idiot? He's two months old. Do you want him to choke? I suppose next thing you'll be tossing him the car keys so he can get himself some takeaway?'

You'll notice from the above examples that drones must always resort to 'the question':

'Do you think ... ?'

'Is he ... ?'

'Should I ... ?'

'What about ... ?'

Mum, however, *knows*. In her world, a world full of hormones, there are *no* alternatives. There is simply what is 'right', 'correct', 'naturally, you idiot' and what is 'bleedingly obvious to anyone with half a brain' — which clearly isn't dopey Daddy!

Chapter 2

Morning Sickness versus Hangover

'Morning sickness': can there be a worse phrase for the expectant mother? (Well, yes, there can be … how about 'thirty-hour labour'? Not to mention, 'Looks like we'll have to perform that episiotomy after all!' … If you need to look it up pal, I suggest you do it fast and discreetly and then you'll know why men don't give birth!)

Morning sickness is something you'll need to come to terms with pretty quickly because if you don't, not only will its debilitating effects bring down your partner, but could very well bring down your entire relationship! Why? Because it's your fault!

That's right … *you* are to blame for the fact that she wakes up each day feeling like she's eaten a tub

IT'S MY ROLE AS A SOON-TO-BE DAD TO EMBRACE FLUID RETENTION AND MORNING SICKNESS...
GOLDIN

of warm fat with a hair in it. And you had better (and quickly) show the appropriate level of concern and contrition to appease the suffering woman.

Contrition? That's right. You need to show not only compassion for her plight but also demonstrate how sorry you are for what *you've* done. You must be a strong and considerate male, one who takes full responsibility for *your* actions (and her state), because that's what she wants.

There can never be enough grovelling, submission and tugging the forelock to make up for the fact that *you* are responsible for her delicate situation. Forget that 'the biological clock was ticking'. Forget that she'd 'always wanted children'. Forget that it 'takes two to tango'. Forget that she told you it would be all right 'just this once' ... or whatever it was that got you into this predicament. Now that it has happened it's all *your* fault.

Whenever good aspects of pregnancy and parenting are discussed or experienced it will always be: aren't 'we' good; aren't 'we' clever; and look what 'we've' done. Whenever it's bad — morning sickness, bloated ankles, sore back, stretch marks, thirty-hour labour and episiotomy — then it is invariably *your* fault.

While some women suffer for months on end and sometimes their entire pregnancy with morning sickness (brought about due to changes in hormonal levels and other stuff specific to chicks), for most women it is an uncomfortable period that lasts only a few weeks.

And while you may feel you've never had to deal with such a sickness before, the good thing is that in all likelihood it *is* something you're all too familiar with. Believe it or not you will be able to empathise because these are experiences and sensations that any 'real' bloke has felt and suffered numerous times! It's just a matter of adjusting your perspective.

You see, for most women 'morning sickness' is nothing more than an appropriately sweet and lacy, chick-speak way of saying 'hangover'! That's right, a brain-splitting, artery-bursting, pounding, nauseating, bloody great hangover!

Now, on the surface, I grant you this may seem unkind, but look at the things common to women who suffer morning sickness. And no, I don't mean the out-of-control hormones — I mean the *real* causes. You see, once pregnant, a lot of women give up, all at once, most of the normal things that make life bearable, like smoking, caffeine, alcohol and late nights. For many women morning sickness has *nothing* to do with their uterus preparing for the foetus; it is simply a case of horrendous cold turkey on a stupendous scale, their bodies writhing in massive shock.

Let's face it, giving up a single vice is hard for the body to handle. Have you tried to give up cigarettes? What about caffeine? It's not a pleasant thing to go through. Imagine what it would be like to all of a sudden give up everything ... at once! The human body is not built to go through this much suffering ... certainly not the male body. This, therefore, is clearly another reason why men don't have babies. We could never handle the detox!

I WANTED TO FIND THE RIGHT TIME TO TELL YOU...
BUNGY JUMPING

Chapter 3

'I'm Pregnant!'

If you are yet to receive 'the announcement' from your partner, you should be aware that a complete parallel universe exists, a universe you are probably oblivious of. Thousands upon thousands of people inhabit it; they walk past you every day and you never see them — or the multitudinous paraphernalia they must drag along. Let me explain.

New, or soon-to-be fathers must quickly come to terms with a life they have never imagined because most men never spend much time 'visualising' themselves as a parent, probably no more time than it takes to rip the top from a cold bottle of beer. Instead, we men spend our time visualising important stuff: the perfect hole-in-one; driving the fastest Formula One lap at Monaco; and being invited to the female showers by an entire cheerleading squad. Unfortunately, while we're visualising ourselves sudsing eighteen firm, flexible, gigglingly free-spirited young women naive in the ways of love, chicks are 'daydreaming' ... daydreaming about babies.

Of course, as soon as a chick utters the phrase 'You're going to be a father', the visualisation ends and reality begins. Bye-bye cheerleaders, hello maternity smock! ('Smock'? Welcome to the pregnant woman's little black dress! There's an entire vocabulary of words you'll need to learn, many of which are designed to make horrible things sound nice.)

Welcome to the 'other side'. When my wife made 'the announcement', this parallel universe just opened up and swallowed me right there and then. She said 'I'm pregnant', and all of a sudden the world was filled with babies and parents and prams. And there was no easing into it either. No dipping of the toe. Just a huge whoosh! From that very moment 'we' decided like rational adults that 'I' really needed to go and have a stiff drink at our nearest bar (and doesn't 'we need a drink' disappear from the vocabulary quickly?!), as we stepped into the street outside our house ... Wham!

Babies! Parents! Prams! It's a terrifying revelation. Remember the movie *The Sixth Sense?* You're like that frightened child protectively pulling the sheets up under your chin, a trembling whisper upon your lips ... 'I see babies. They're everywhere and I don't even know where they came from.'

It's like buying a brand new model car that nobody has yet ... until you drive from the showroom onto roads choked with them! Let's face it, for most men prior to this moment, experiences with pregnant women or children are limited to only two situations:

1 Pointing at the extended bellies of women you know at work and saying a cheery 'Hey! Wow! Congratulations!' (hoping they aren't just struggling with 'fluid retention' ... whatever the hell that is); or
2 Pretending to show enthusiasm while holding someone else's kid (at an awkward arm's-length kind of distance, all the while trying to avoid being smeared by drool or snot). And then afterwards saying witty, sniggering things to your friends about the shape of the baby's head or the size of its ears.

Well ... all that changes!

I honestly believe that the majority of men have never known or noticed this parallel universe. Psychologists say this is not unusual; it is linked to the well-documented male condition 'domestic blindness'. For most men this condition is another simple survival technique. They don't see the dirt, dust and grime building up around the house ... and therefore it doesn't exist! In acute cases, however, its effects can be debilitating. Some men can open a fridge or cupboard door, blankly stare in and if they can't see what they want ... *then it's time for take-away*! Some men even lose total use of their arms and are unable to move things aside on the refrigerator shelves to view what might be hidden behind the milk or the three-week-old KFC. My mother and my wife have always been able to extract things I swear weren't there when I looked twenty seconds earlier!

You know, there are whole aisles in supermarkets and whole sections in chemists devoted to nothing but baby stuff? Well there are! In fact, there are entire magazines, whole shops ... a complete industry devoted to nothing but babies. Truly! And what great businesses they are. Imagine operating a business where anyone who enters cannot leave without buying something! Honestly it cannot be done.

These businesses have harnessed an unseen force — some rogue law of nature. If you don't believe me, stand outside one (not too close in case you get sucked in), and see if you can spot anyone leaving without having made a purchase.

Don't be fooled by those men exiting without

something in their arms. Watch and wait. They're simply moving their car closer to the store. They'll soon head back in, only to reappear with a couple of shop assistants pushing a trolley groaning under the weight of purchases. These they will try to stuff into the vehicle under the steely command of a pregnant woman with whom no one is going to argue.

As you continue your reconnaissance, observe the expressions on the faces of the men as they stumble around. There they are, piled up with arms full of baby 'stuff', valiantly trying to give their partners the appearance of being interested and supportive. Notice the dazed and confused shuffling? Notice the glazed eyes that look but don't see? Watch as they try to send pleading looks towards other men, hoping that one of them is strong enough to assist in this crisis, but only to receive the same glassy stare mirrored back; the only acknowledgement an eyes-down nod of the head, as they trail like cowed dogs behind their wives or girlfriends. It's shell shock! Just like those poor lost souls from the Western Front, broken by the unrelenting barrage of an enemy assault.

You see, this is a *special kind* of shopping with a woman. This isn't the endless tedium of visiting clothing store after clothing store staffed by vacuous and obnoxious shop assistants; shops blaring with techno music; shops with no chairs to sit on while you wait for your lady to decide she doesn't like any of the fifteen different items she's taken into the changing room.

No, this isn't the thrill or frenzy of 'therapy shopping' where women have to spend money on more dresses, more shoes and more make-up or they'll 'just die of embarrassment being seen in public'. Oh no! This is different. This is *really* serious. This is 'power shopping'.

Money is to be spent ... money *must* be spent — but not with a reckless and joyful abandon. This is shopping that *must* be done ... and done right! And so women stride into 'Baby Lands' ... capable, confident and determined. Picking things up. Putting them down. Looking. Squeezing. Shaking. Comparing ... Asking questions! You see in Baby Lands normal rules do not apply. This is because *they* have the hormones ... and we don't. Here men cannot rationalise. Here men may not haggle.

Once inside Baby Lands there is no debate. Here you have no say, no control (particularly over your wallet!). Upon entering Baby Lands a vortex envelops you ... and it can only be cleared by spending money. There simply is no other escape.

In Baby Lands there are endless things on the shelves, the showroom floor and in the window that you *will* need, that you *do* not have, and that you *cannot* improvise for. 'Fair enough,' you think to yourself. 'This is a baby after all and it has specific needs.' This is rational, logical and sensible thinking.

The real problem is that as you look around you begin to notice there's all this *other* stuff. This is stuff you *don't* need, *won't* require and *can* do without, however, *this is an 'emotional' time*! You see, if it has cute pictures of animals or dangly bits or lace, then you're going to be walking out of the store with an armload of it because 'I'm pregnant'. (And if you thought 'they' were emotional before pregnancy, then you ain't seen nothing yet! Remember the hormones!)

'OK,' you say to yourself. 'I accept I'll have to part with the cash for essentials and possibly a couple of cuddly little things we could survive without, but surely this is not enough to reduce grown men to these empty, hollow shells I see shuffling before me?'

And quite right you are because there is more … Remember when I said these were great businesses? Here's the real reason why you should invest heavily in Baby Lands shares and options: not only do you *have* to spend money *every time* you enter, but you are 'morally obligated' to buy the best–safest–softest–strongest and therefore … ? That's right … the most expensive! Here's an example.

At some stage of the pregnancy, as our baby developed happily inside its mother's belly, my wife pronounced that today was the day we must purchase a high chair. Now rationally I could have debated that the child wouldn't require a high chair until some months after it was born, but I had learned that when my wife made a 'baby statement' she was right and I might as well agree enthusiastically and supportively because ... ? Yep, *she* has the hormones and *I* don't ... therefore what the hell would I know anyway? Pregnancy is no place for ridiculous male rationality and reason! *How* she knew exactly when these things were necessary is beyond me but she did ... and I quickly learned not to argue. (It only prolonged the inevitable purchase and it was better to get the pain over with swiftly.)

And while they may be irrational, women have plenty of rat cunning because the other reason men are dragged along on these occasions is so that in the future, if there's something wrong with the chair or you stupidly complain one night about how much it cost, then you can quickly be put in your place with a, 'Well, you were there. You should have noticed. Why didn't you speak up?' (suggesting you had some control or say in the decision at the time, which obviously you didn't!).

So, we arrived at Baby Lands. My wife strode in. Purposeful. Powerful. I entered the store and the familiar feeling of being overwhelmed, of hopelessness, rushed in on me. Taking a breath to steady my nerves, I looked around and saw in the middle of the store the long row of high chairs neatly displayed, one against the other in various colours and shapes and sizes and ... prices.

High chairs, of course, are nothing any 'normal' pre-parent male has any idea about. Therefore, as I would approach any unknown and potentially dangerous animal, I carefully, warily, sized them up.

From a distance, downwind, I stood motionless and observed them. Then with an extended open palm to show them I was friendly, I slowly moved closer. I gave one a nudge, a push. It didn't attack. Feeling a little more confident I extended a finger and lifted one by the tray onto its back legs. It remained docile. So I became a little more robust. Trying to look as if I knew what I was doing I pushed one back and forth a few times on its wheels and in case anyone was watching, gave a thoughtful, knowing nod, before moving onto the next one.

Nothing to it, I thought. This baby stuff is easy. So as a normal, healthy and intelligent male, I *sensibly* walked down the row to the cheaper (although I prefer the term 'inexpensive') end. I *rationalised* they all have to pass basic standards, standards debated and deeply considered by government experts who know about these things — so why pay more money than necessary, right? That's when I noticed my wife and the shop assistant (or, if you prefer, 'the enemy' — the assistant, my wife, or both, take your pick) at the other, pricy end of the display.

I heard the assistant say phrases like: 'Well, you really can't put a price on your child's comfort and safety can you?', and 'Sure, they all pass the basic standards but … '. But!? But what?!

Yes, all of them have to, *must* pass the basic standards, so what else is there to know? Plenty, according to *the enemy*, and before I realised what had happened I was standing at the check-out offering my credit card for the most expensive high chair on display! How did this happen?

Admittedly, there are different features and things to look for, but do you end up buying the most expensive high chair because of safety? No. Comfort? No. Gold plating? (Well on some models possibly, but not in this instance.) No, the real reason you pay the equivalent of the Paraguayan national deficit for a chair your child will smear with Vegemite and vomit, is because of nothing less than *peer group pressure* and emotional blackmail.

This is the all-powerful and overwhelming universal force these businesses have harnessed, and which makes owning stocks in Baby Lands more valuable than diamonds, gold or oil shares. Here's how it works:

1 You really, really want your wife's continued approval of you as someone responsible enough to be a parent. This is something you know she's been constantly watching and critically assessing since announcing the pregnancy and you know this is one of those occasions where you need to pass the examination; and
2 You and your wife are in a store filled with other people and even though they're total strangers, you *both* really, really want their approval of you as people responsible enough to be parents. You can't be certain, but you get the feeling that every one of them is constantly watching and critically assessing your purchases, and this is one of those occasions where you need to pass the examination.

So sure they all pass the basic standards ... but do you want to be seen in public with anything that loudly says you could possibly be compromising your child's safety or comfort, just for the sake of something as shallow as money? So beware. In Baby Lands there is no such thing as 'popping in for a look' or 'just browsing thanks'. There is only 'Will that be cash or credit, sir?'

I WAS HOPING FOR A PRAM THAT EMBODIED FERRARI'S 'PRANCING HORSE'... BUT ALL I GOT WAS THE 'PRANCE'!
GOLDING

Chapter 4

Pram Envy

On one notable occasion I was at least allowed some dignity regarding a purchase for our baby. It was a one off when I actually appeared to take control, where I made a choice and, as a result, was briefly granted some amount of self-respect as a man. This was the day my wife announced, 'We have to buy a pram!'

As the months had gone by since the announcement, I'd started to take some notice of what was going on around me. I also knew this day would come, and I was worried. Not only is a pram one of the *bigger* purchases — a fleet of brand new Korean cars with three years' warranty costs less — I also knew there was a bewildering variety from which to choose. And to me, all the choices looked bad. (No matter what kind of pram it is, it's always going to look a little emasculating.)

So there we were at 'Pramtastic', a subsidiary of Baby Lands. We are looking at prams and I have that familiar feeling of having been freshly neutered. (As usual, I've been dragged along and I'm trying to be 'supportive' — again that term you need to learn fast, or find out how it really does feel to be gelded!). As usual there were hundreds of prams in all colours and designs and styles ... and, of course, prices. As I look around though, one thing seemed consistent. They were all a little 'feminine'. A touch 'girly'. A bit 'nancy'.

There's prams with pretty floral patterns and ones with teddy bears; some have lace trims, others have hoods covered in butterflies and many have white wheels. It's all a bit too 'bunny-wunnies' for my liking. Sure there's the trendy, three-wheel-jogging-type prams, but unless you're wearing lycra and sweatbands and actually jogging (never seen anyone yet), well, you look a bit naff. And you see, we'd already checked it out and knew the stork would be delivering a little 'boy' bundle of joy.

'Is this what my son wants to be seen in?' I thought to myself. 'More importantly, is this what I want to be seen in public with? What will my mates think?'

I began to get fidgety. Then, ominously, the good lady wife started seriously checking out one of those high-rise contraptions — the big antique looking ones with huge white wheels! I actually heard the sales assistant say, 'Just like Mary Poppins', and the two of them smiled. A catastrophe was unfolding before me.

A decision was about to be made without my involvement because of a silent yet shared female moment, one in which no words need be said but there is clear understanding between them. Like a Vulcan mind meld, they each know the other had played dress ups with dolls, been to pyjama parties, read *Anne of Green Gables*, novels by the Brontë sisters, and believe that out there, somewhere, there really is a man they would 'swoon' over ('Swoon?' 'Swoooooooon' ... Stupid sounding word!). In unison they turned and looked at me with disdain and the shop assistant gave my wife a reassuring 'Sure, he's no Mr D'arcy but then who is?'

This was something unexpected. As if the peer pressure and emotional blackmail wasn't enough, my wife was now exhibiting all traits of the psychosis 'pram envy'! She was seriously contemplating the worst possible pram of all time. The girliest, prettiest, white-wheeled pram ever made. And it was big — it demanded attention. This was a conspicuous perambulator!

Not only could I not stand the thought of being

seen in public with this myself, I knew my son would blame me forever when photos of him in such a contrivance were passed around at his twenty-first birthday party, and any time a potential 'wife' was brought home to meet the parents.

Tension flooded me. I had to do something ... but what? Then ... in my darkest moment, I saw it ... Standing in a corner of the shop away from the other prams, high upon a pedestal all its own, gleaming and shiny, with spotlights and funky background music was the 'Man Pram'!

The Man Pram is a wonder of masculine ingenuity, design and engineering. The Bang & Olufsen of babydom. Stainless steel and powder coated black metal finish. Blue and black washable trim with silver reflector strips. Big knobbly wheels and not the trendy three-wheel-jogging thing but four. Four big knobbly rubber wheels. With real tread! (And they're inflatable. You have to use a service station air hose to pump these mothers up.) Rubber grips on the handles. Air bags. Bassinets that lock in, seats that latch out, speed stripes, washable removable material that looks high tech. Hell, this thing even has suspension settings to adjust as junior gains weight, and it converts to a stroller for when the kid gets older!

I dragged my wife over and enthusiastically,

maniacally started showing her all the different features and aspects of this wonderful vehicle. She maintained a stern face and looked back lovingly at the Mary Poppins pram. Then she glanced at Man Pram's price tag and raised a questioning eyebrow. It is by far the most expensive pram ever constructed but I was desperate. I laughed off the price!

'Do you think I'm so shallow as to be concerned about price at a time like this?' … I heard myself say in some strange distant echo, that, even as the words left my lips, I was surprised I'd spoken.

She looked me up and down coolly. Sternly. Once again she stared longingly at the white-wheeled wonder, paused for a long moment and grimly nodded her consent that we may purchase the Man Pram.

'Thank you, thank you,' I cried, falling to one knee and kissing her hand as she brushed past me to investigate scented nappy buckets. Then you know what? It wasn't until we were back in the car with the Man Pram all boxed up and she was quietly smiling and humming to herself that it dawned on me. It had been just a little too easy to convince her. She was a little *too* swift to give up on the big-wheeled girly number, and then I remembered … pram envy! The realisation slammed into my brain. She'd checked it all out beforehand! Man Pram was the pram she had wanted all along, but she knew full well I'd baulk at the price if she just rushed straight to it!

Damn she's good! Like Montgomery and Rommel in the deserts of North Africa, you have to respect an adversary when they exhibit such sheer audacity and tactical brilliance. I've got to say though, now that we're stuck with it, Man Pram is a pretty impressive machine. This is a pram you can stand around and look at with your mates. One you can admire even while cooking a BBQ.

'Sure mate, check out the suspension and the adjustable grip bar for the kid! Get a load of the detachable hood, mozzie net and wind break attachment. She's a beauty.'

'Bet it cost you a pretty penny?'

'Sure did!' you say, puffed up and confident. Then, with a dry, perfectly charred sausage gripped firmly between the tongs in one hand, a stubby of beer in the other, you look your men friends in the eye and say, 'Remember this though. Any old pram will pass the basic standards, but you just can't put a price on your kid's comfort and safety can you? Cheers!'

Chapter 5

Birth

There are no words to describe the elation you feel when a brand new baby is placed into your arms. It is simply sensory overload. Before that moment, however, is the birth itself!

Now whether you want to be at the birth or not, it probably has very little to do with you anyway. This is another of those areas where your partner will decide ... and you'll do as you're told. (Unless it's one of those 'backseat of the car on the way to the hospital' occasions, in which case, like it or not, you'll be up to your elbows in it — literally!)

These days there's an enormous amount of pressure on men to be at the actual birthing event. Looking back through the ages this is a relatively new requirement for we drones and a lot of this pressure is more to do with what everybody else

TIPS FOR SUPPORTIVE PARTNERS IN THE BIRTHING SUITE... DON'T WEAR KILTS!
GOLDING

considers best, not necessarily the mum and dad-to-be. Of course, plenty of expectant dads do want to be there but, like the whole nappy changing thing, there's a lot of men who aren't totally ecstatic about the 'blood and guts' part, yet feel almost shamed into attending the birth. ('Attending the birth'? Sounds like opening night at the opera!)

Let's face it, forget the guys ... many women don't want to have to go through the experience either! Personally, I was never too thrilled with the idea. I mean here we are, brought up all our lives to be the hunters, the protectors, the ones to stand boldly in the face of danger, who slay the mighty dragon that threatens to hurt our lady loves. Yet we are expected to be present at what could be the most gruesome experience any of us ever go through, all the while unable to really do anything useful to assist our woman. So, whatever your opinion, it is accepted that, for most men, being at the birth is compulsory, therefore look at it as another opportunity to be 'supportive'.

This particular kind of support involves assuming the position of convenient punching bag, allowing the living flesh to be torn from any body part that can be flayed at by the 'little lady' and, of course, meekly submitting to the most profane language and abuse for being the cause of what, you've got to admit, looks like a bloody uncomfortable process!

How any of us survive the birthing process is beyond me — is it any wonder we don't remember going through it ourselves? There you are gently bobbing about in a dark, warm and watery environment with the pleasing sounds of your mother's heart rhythmically beating away, intermingled with the funny gurgling sounds of massive indigestion when, all of a sudden, your world is literally turned inside out.

The water gushes away and you are tortuously squeezed from all directions. Then, if things don't move along fast enough, cold metal doovers and rubber-gloved hands start reaching out and having a tug at you. If that fails, you may suffer the indignity of having a suction cup applied to your head and being literally dragged out into the world like something nasty that's fallen down the sink and been sucked up with a plunger!

Then there's the rush of freezing air, the bright lights, the tubes shoved up your nose and down your throat and maybe a slap on the arse for good measure. All the mucus and goop and blood is rubbed off your brand new delicate skin with a rough towel (it doesn't matter how soft and fluffy they are ... from where you've just come it's got to feel coarse). You're laid out, naked and exposed, measured and weighed before being wrapped up so tight you can't move a limb (even if you knew how, which you don't). You start to experience hunger for the first time because up until now the food's been coming to you automatically, while your unfocused eyes see nothing but weird blurs. *Of course* we don't remember. Why would we want to? Something that traumatic must take years to get over. Anyway, back to *attending the birth*.

To tell the truth, I liked the old 1950s Desi and Lucy type of birthing experience. You know, hanging around the waiting room with a couple of other harried and nervous looking blokes, smoking cigarettes and pacing a lot; thin black tie pulled loose from the collar of a white business shirt. Hands constantly run through Brylcreemed hair. Waiting for that gentle, motherly type of nurse to come along, give a knowing smile and lead you by the hand to look through the glass at a sweetly slumbering baby, all puffed up and wrapped in clean white swaddling.

Why be subjected to the little purply-blue crying thing all covered in white fatty stuff and blood? After all, you want a baby — a nice looking baby, like the ones in the movies. Not a slime-covered reptile. Or would you prefer something more dramatic and triumphant? A touch of something epic, like in the old gladiator movies?

The baby is brought to you upon a hilltop and laid at your feet in the cold and misty pre-dawn air. Just like Caesar, your mates, the Praetorian guards, whisper in your ear, 'Don't touch it. Don't acknowledge it I beg of thee!' Then, brushing your minders aside with an imperious sweep of your arm, you would bellow, 'Move away thy caring but base and foolish fellows!' And as the first golden lance of morning sunlight stabs the heavens, you bend down and gently lift the baby into your arms. Slowly, raising it high above your head, you turn to the ecstatic assembled masses below and loudly, exultantly, proclaim into the nearest forum, your voice choked with emotion, 'I am a father!' And as the crowd roars and claps and stamps its approval, the sounds of trumpets and drums fill the air, and flocks of perfectly white doves flutter skyward.

Strangely, it wasn't quite like that for us.

In fact, 'we' both wimped out on the 'natural' part of it. 'We' had an 'elective' caesarean. Yep, we actually 'booked' the birth — just like going away for the weekend.

'I see we have a vacancy on February the 19th Mr and Mrs Storey. The weather for giving birth is lovely that time of year.'

That's right, not unlike having a mole or a blemish removed! Rather than being 'born' we chose to have our son 'extracted'. As my wife's favourite T-shirt proudly proclaims, she was 'Too Posh to Push'!

'But what about "bonding" with the baby?', I hear the screaming mung-bean munchers cry out in anguish. Give me a break! With all baby goes through just getting out of there the natural way, it's hardly going to remember or care whether Daddy was 'attending' in the corner of the operating theatre (I mean *birthing suite*), a trembling, teary eyed, blithering wreck, reduced to a quivering mess by the emotion of the moment ... and the pain inflicted on him by his partner.

And, as for new-age umbilical-cord cutters, listen, if the child was capable of giving a damn, think about how much you're going to have to fork out for in therapy when repressed memories swell to the surface of its consciousness ... and the first to return is a blurred vision of Daddy in a surgical mask leaning over it with a pair of scissors!

Of course the whole ability to give birth is a special 'gift' of nature granted to women — 'nature' realising pretty swiftly that if it was up to men the species would not have survived beyond Adam! This is what most of us fellas struggle to understand: if there are alternatives to the blood and guts, tearing, cutting and stitching (there's that 'episiotomy' thing again), why would anyone in their right mind want to go through it?

Medical science has managed to do away with all kinds of nastiness in our lives — like polio for instance. Nobody gets on their soapbox crying out that the eradication of infectious disease is a bad thing, yet when it comes to child birthing 'options' there is strident resistance to anything that's deemed 'not natural'. Why?

The answer would appear to be a chick version of 'real men don't eat quiche'. 'Real' women don't have caesareans (or if they do, only as a life-saving last resort!). There is a very definite, though never spoken of, secret social hierarchy between the sisters — a ranking system of achievement.

'Real' chicks, the ones atop the birthing strata, are those whose labour lasts for about 300 hours. These are the 'super birthers' who, through much tearing, cutting and subsequent stitching, stoically give birth to babies half the size of tip trucks without drugs or assistance, and if you ask them they'll proudly show you the battle scars to prove it! To most men's thinking, they're to be admired but only in the same way we admire heavyweight boxers: they're impressive to watch but you'd be out of your skull to jump in the ring with one.

Next rung down are the 'earth mother natural birthers' who manage to push out a baby with little

SUPER BIRTHERS
GOLDING

or no effort at all. A few quick breaths, a pelvic squeeze or two and 'Welcome!' to the newest member of the human race. These are the women who went to the edge, prepared to do battle but the enemy gave up with little or no resistance. 'Oh, that's *fortunate*,' say the super birthers between jealous, gritted teeth.

A bit further down the birthing pecking order are women who are psychotically desperate to go down the natural path. They engage the enemy in a pitched battle, fighting and struggling until both forces are exhausted and a 'Pyrrhic victory' is declared by the closest doctor, midwife or psychiatrist before they are 'forced' to undergo a caesar. 'Oh, what a *shame*,' say the super birthers between jealous, gritted teeth.

Finally, a long, long way behind — in some families the shame is too great to speak about for generations to come — are women, like my wife, who choose a caesar. 'Oh, that's *pathetic*', say super birthers between jealous, gritted teeth.

Why is it that so many women are still prepared to go through with a 'natural' birth? It would appear the reason is an unwritten code in which a woman must always tell other women that it's 'not so bad', that moments after the baby is delivered (even as the doctor is 'tidying up down there'), the pain is miraculously forgotten in an overwhelming wave of euphoric love for the baby.

Now call me cynical … but I'm not buying it. It sounds very similar to an all too frequent male condition known as '*lying your arse off to avoid humiliation*'. Let me give you an example.

Never in the entire history of the human race has there been a documented instance of a bloke jumping into a swimming pool, water hole, dam, lake, river or ocean surf, bobbing back up to the surface and saying to his friends, 'Hey, don't do it guys, don't come in! It's bloody freezing!'

All males, no matter what society they live in, at one time or another, have stupidly jumped into water they thought would be pleasant only to feel their skin crackle and their muscles spasm as hypothermia sets in. Yet immediately on breaking the surface these same men will swim and splash around like demented dolphins in a vain effort to stay warm and convince their friends to follow them into the water, thus washing away their own potential humiliation at being an idiot. 'Yeah, come on in. The water's fine!' they say. 'Trust me!'

So it is with the sisters.

'Of course you'll give birth naturally! Hurt? Pain? Tearing and stitches? You won't even remember it. Trust me!'

latte
decaf latte
soy latte
baby latte
GOLDING

Chapter 6

Breasts

Bet you couldn't wait to get to this chapter? In fact, you may have just picked the book up in-store and flicked to this page (after checking no one was watching), to see if it would be any good. A book for blokes needs a chapter on breasts right?

No, you're right, it probably doesn't, so I really need to confess. I just wrote this chapter heading to ensure I got sales. There is nothing I can say to those of you who have paid up front, walked out of the bookstore and opened directly to this chapter except, 'I'm sorry.' I feel bad. I've let you down but hell I've got a family to feed and I hope you'll forgive me. Check out some of the other chapters though ... you might find *something of interest*.

WE'VE GOT FULL CREAM, SOY, LIGHT, FAT REDUCED, OR HELEN...
MILK
MILK
GOLDING

Chapter 7

More Breasts

OK, well, they said if I *didn't* do something on breasts they weren't going to publish the book at all. They didn't want to be sued for fraud and anyway, the publisher said he got really annoyed when he immediately flipped to the 'Breasts' chapter while perusing the manuscript. He said it was 'false, misleading and deceptive'.

'Not unlike a good many breasts themselves,' I added.

'Just write something,' he said — no sense of humour these people!

The main point to make about breasts is this: enjoy them while you can! You see, your partner's breasts are about to become something like public property and, if you're the kind of guy that gets a little jealous and irritable when someone else is just taking a discreet peak at your partner's bosom, then you'd better take a few moments to come to terms with this issue.

Your partner's breasts or — as you may be used to thinking of them — *your* breasts, are now openly looked at, talked about and discussed. You may need to become knowledgeable about such mysterious things as 'cup' size (or at least learn when to nod at the appropriate point in a conversation regarding such matters).

Other people will talk about 'your' breasts. Practical strangers will openly ask, 'Have they become bigger?', 'Are they harder?', 'Do they hurt?', and 'Do they leak?' And that's just the tame stuff before the baby is born. Wait till the discussion turns to 'blocked ducts' and 'Is there blood in the milk?' Even the strongest of men would crumble!

For example, my wife is fairly discreet about her breasts, where she does and doesn't expose them ... and to whom! Yet about an hour after the baby was born, while my wife was understandably in a state of distraction and exhaustion, this complete stranger, a woman called a midwife, walked into our room and without any great ceremony or approval, grabbed my wife's breasts!

Normally, for a healthy male, this should have been an exciting and possibly sensual development worth recording on film, but no! This woman simply started to 'knead' my wife's breasts. And while, for some time, I had been enthralled and mindlessly excited by the size and firmness of my wife's newly engorged decolletage — her 'big boosies' if you prefer — this woman came along and simply grabbed at them with all the enthusiasm of a fishmonger grappling a dead cod.

'Hang on,' I thought, 'Those are *my* breasts!' Strangely enough, I found out from my wife afterwards, that this was the same thought she was having. Prior to this time my wife and I had speculated on the bovine nature of breastfeeding ('Oh look darling, it's all so "cow" like. God, I think we'll go straight to the bottle!'), but now we were slammed confrontingly back to nature.

Meanwhile, our tiny baby was lying quietly in his mother's arms trying to get over the rigorous workout of having just been born (well, OK ... extracted), and now found himself with a hand firmly applied to the back of the head, his face pushed into an enormous breast while a big nipple was slipped into his mouth. Not surprisingly he gagged at the indignity of such disrespectful and obviously discomforting behaviour, pulled back as best he could and protested that he didn't like being pushed about.

His parents — the people who should rightly have sprung to his defence — were still dazed and addlepated by the events of the day that had presented 'Pink and Wrinkly' to us. We were dumbly and uselessly watching on as the midwife simply forced his tiny face back onto his mother's breast, this time squeezing his jaw and forcing his lips to accommodatingly slide over the nipple again. Just before his little mouth grabbed hold I'm sure I saw him glare at me with unfocused eyes and a look of, 'Yeah, big help in life you'll be. Thanks for nothing pal!'

Then, before we knew it, he 'latched on' (another phrase to learn and then knowingly and thoughtfully nod at during baby conversations), and our baby started contentedly suckling away.

'Wow. How cool is that?' his deliriously happy parents thought. Mrs 'Seen it all before AND I'm well over it' then left us to get on with being a family. Which was just perfect until the little pig had taken so much milk in he retched up three quarters all over his adoring mother. (Welcome to baby vomit — but more about that later!)

So this was the start of the family feud over just whose breasts were they anyway. The baby *needed* them, I *wanted* them and Mum was threatening to have them removed altogether.

At this point you may wish to add the terms

'cracked nipples' and 'mastitis' to your list of 'why men don't give birth and why we don't "suckle"'. ('Suckle', now there's another of those nice sounding words that masks something which, in reality, is bad.)

You see, after a few months, feeding the little beast every two to three hours begins taking its toll (yes pal, EVERY two to three HOURS — it's not a typo and no, nobody told me either!) I felt like the living dead and can't imagine what my wife was going through.

For some women, even several regular feeding sessions a day isn't enough to drain away all the milk they're producing. In fact, when a baby cries it triggers physiological responses in mothers that stimulate milk production and breasts can, all by themselves, begin leaking! To avoid the dam bursting, so to speak, pressure needs to be released. So be warned! Do not sneak into the bathroom unannounced as your lady love is showering, just because you feel a bit of 'doctors and nurses' could be fun. That throbbing strain of built-up tension in your groin disappears mighty fast when you slide back the shower screen door and a stream of warm milk is 'expressed' into your face by a new mum who has been easing some of the built-up pressure she's having to deal with!

As if the expressing, mastitis, leaking, blocked ducts and cracked nipples isn't enough to deal with, along come the baby's teeth! Now, I don't know about your experience with nipples but I've never given too much attention to mine. I've certainly never understood the 'sensuality' of dripped candle wax that seems so much a part of 'art' movies. (Sure you might think my sex life is missing something special but like Mongolian horsemen who play polo with sheep heads as pucks, there are some experiences in life I'm prepared to live without.) And, while I love my child to unplumbed depths, I can't imagine my wife's love for him — as she had to place her inflamed and bruised nipples between jaws filling with razor sharp teeth several times a day!

Eventually, even love has its limits and Mum decided to turn off the faucet. This, however, is not something Mum actually controls. Bosoms used to being sucked dry several times a day continue to fill. Therefore they require regular 'tapping' and if you thought breast-feeding itself was a little back to nature, wait till you get a look at the technology of a breast pump in action!

At least this isn't one of those things that gets a fancy title to make it sound nicer than it is. This is a tool! A pump! A pump for extracting milk from your partner's breasts so it can be fed to junior through a bottle later. Yep, just like down on the farm, Jethro!

As I said earlier, this book isn't designed to tell you *everything*, but rather to warn you in advance about some of the stuff that comes with fatherhood. So, I'll leave it to you to find out all the reasons why your partner may one day require a regular 'siphoning'. To give you an idea though, a friend relates her story of attending a high profile executive meeting. She had just returned from maternity leave and wondered why the fifteen men she was addressing were unable to hold eye contact with her and awkwardly fidgeted throughout the entire presentation, until she looked down and saw two enormous wet patches slowly spreading out across her brand new power suit!

So, believe it or not, a day may very well come when you and your wife will be chatting away in the normal manner couples do and you will no longer notice she is rhythmically squeezing a handle attached to a suction device squirting milk from her engorged bosom into a container, the contents of which are then poured into a satchel, sealed and added to the growing number of frozen human milk pouches you now keep in the freezer, alongside the peas and ice-cream.

'I see the price of oil has risen again.'

Squirt, squirt, squirt.

'Oh really?'

Squirt.

'Yes, but gold is holding steady.'

Squirt, squirt, squirt.

'Well that's good to hear.'

Squirt, squirt.

And here's another day to keep an eye out for. It happened with our baby at about the three-month mark. We finally felt under control enough with the new situation to have a few friends around for a BBQ. What were we thinking? As it turned out we weren't. We were so sleep deprived (or is that depraved?) that we weren't thinking at all.

As our friends played 'pass the baby' (and, for our sakes, pretended to really love being around a baby for the first time in the twenty years we'd all known each other), our son dug his hungry little face into the breasts of my mate's brand new, 'first-time-meeting-his-friends' girlfriend. With a laugh, she gently pulled bub away and lied to us all that she didn't mind the drool mark left on her expensive new silk top.

And wasn't this a revelation to junior? I'd noticed, as the months had passed, that our baby's eyes were obviously beginning to focus better and, as I took him from her, he looked around the group and I swear I could hear his little mind say, ‘You mean they’re everywhere? Every second person’s got ’em? Wow!’

During this period however, remember one thing: that day you think you’re under control, that it’s time to invite people around for a few drinks and ‘meet the baby’, sit down and try to really figure out between the two of you if you truly are up to it. Maybe ring some family or friends and ask their thoughts because sleep deprivation can make you do some silly things.

For instance, your best mate might not be able to forgive you too soon for reducing that same new girlfriend to the trembling point of hysteria when she looks down and realises the tinkling sound, from the refreshingly cold glass of gin and tonic you just handed her, is not the ice cubes bobbing about in her drink, but rather a couple of satchels of your partner’s freshly tapped and snap-frozen boob juice!

WHAT IS IT, LASSIE... IS LITTLE STEVIE IN TROUBLE?

Chapter 8

Nappies

Firstly, why aren't they called *crappies* because that's what they are? Do you know the worst thing about nappies? It's not what ends up in them, but that men are now expected to get in there and deal with it! Maybe you ought to grab a beer and take a big swig before reading on.

Think about this ... Nappy changing is something no other generation of men before us has ever been expected to do. Sure, a few hairy, lefty, chanting, dope smokin', cheese-cloth wearing, commune living, tree hugging, proto-anti-globalisation-1960s-hippy-types gave it a go ... but no one took them seriously. No one ever believed the day would arrive when men as a whole would ever be expected to change a nappy. That was 'women's work'.

Well, it would appear the chicks have put their

foot down on this one. For most of us, it ain't just 'women's work' any more. But thankfully, 'necessity is the *father* of invention'!

Once it became obvious this jarring shift in Western man's paradigm could not be contained, MAN-kind collectively hitched up his pants, straightened his hat, took a big globby spit in the dirt and prepared to face the daunting task ahead!

You see, it may have been OK for untold centuries for women to grapple with changing, cleaning, folding, washing, and hanging out to dry nappies, but as soon as changing baby came into the realm of beer and cars and sport, then something better had to be found and 'tah-dah!', so it was: the disposable nappy was miraculously unveiled to a stunned and rapturous world.

Now look, this book is designed to assist blokes in the early stages of being a father, so if you are a starting to feel a little bit disturbed by this ... get over it. I know, I know — the environment. Look, I feel bad about it too, but there's no *real* choice.

I will gladly chase down harpoon-wielding whalers in the heaving and freezing seas of the Southern Ocean. I will give to 'Save the Condor', even though it's an ugly bloody bird that eats dead things. I will personally climb the Himalayan mountains and remove other people's waste and trash, but please don't make me give up disposable nappies!

I understand that in six thousand years from now my selfishness will mean all humanity is condemned to living on mountains of toxic plastic and weird unnatural fibres that never break down, but please don't take them away. You see ... babies crap ... a lot!

And I mean a *lot*! And while it's bad enough to be a man and expected to change the baby, it is totally unreasonable to expect us to also grapple with the finer details of folding origami shapes, getting our big man fingers around tiny, springy safety-pin things and then washing, bleaching and hanging them out to dry. This is too much!

And before you go on about the cost of the things and damage to the environment, think about the cost to the environment of all the water required for washing — not to mention the chemicals for cleaning, bleaching and sterilising 'real' nappies. I reckon it's a line-ball call. Oh, and a word of warning if you really are a committed cloth type: don't ever allow yourself even 'just once' to try a disposable, for you too will be seduced by the dark side.

If you're still feeling uncomfortable, your social-enviro-conscience niggling away at the back of your mind, a David Suzuki hypertension starting to constrict your capillaries, remember, it can be expected that you'll have to change somewhere in the vicinity of four thousand nappies! That's four thousand *per baby*. (God forbid you forget what put you in this predicament and go gigglingly back to where any sensible angel would fear to tread without proper precaution or anatomical re-arrangement.) Of that four thousand you can expect up to 50 per cent of the crappies to be filled with something toxic.

Like so much else to do with babies, this is not a situation we men can control. It is entirely up to junior to figure out that there's an alternative to having its bot-bot manhandled several times a day by grown people who really don't want to be there. In some cases it can take up to *four years* before baby realises that Dad (as he holds a pair of legs in the air with one hand and a 'baby wipe' in the other) isn't singing 'Baa Baa Black Sheep' with quite the same gusto as he used to the first several hundred times they shared these particular 'bonding' sessions.

See, whether you use disposable or traditional nappies, the fact is you're going to be spending a lot of time around poo. If you also happen to have a lovable family dog (or as in our case *two*), your life now pretty much revolves around the digestive tract of various animals and what emanates from there! And it comes at you with a rush too, all this poo.

Babies' first nappies are absolutely stupefying because of what's in them. It's called 'meconium' and it's not poo — well, not as you've ever known it. This is the stuff that first comes out of baby. Meconium is more like gooey bitumen or pitch. This is what dinosaurs used to fall into, so be careful when handling it if you don't want to be put on display in a museum 500 years from now with the

label 'Bog Man'! This stuff is thick, black and sticky and lasts for the first few times baby does number twos. Seriously, you could place some small Middle Eastern nation on a couple of meconium filled nappies and they'd be able to drill away at it for decades!

Poo, do-do, ka-ka, crap, number twos, poop, bog, cack — whatever you want to call it — suddenly and unexpectedly fills what must have been a repressed void because it gets talked about so much. It's almost as if you have to make up for not having discussed it previously in your life.

I don't recall ever chatting about the contents of our bowels with my friends during a game of football, with my wife over a romantic candle-lit dinner or with the family gathered at the Christmas table! Yet what's in baby's nappy is an open discussion with anyone at any time in any setting. If you're with another person who has either recently — or 100 years previously — attained membership in the Parenthood Club, then baby's poo is an open-forum discussion.

Everything about it is up for review: the colour, consistency, scent and the amount. It even gets compared! No detail is considered irrelevant — this is vital stuff! My wife and I now have an entire vocabulary to describe and detail what's been going on in junior's shorts when we hand over baby control from one to the other. Just like a swift military debrief or a changing of the guard:

'Has he eaten?'

'Yeah — spaghetti and cheese, oh and some peas.'

'Need changing?'

'Should be OK. I changed one at 0800.'

'Poo?'

'Yeah — yellowy, smooth clay type but with a few lumps. Doesn't smell too bad but lots of it, you know?'

'Yeah, managed to contain and neutralise one of those yesterday morning!'

So what sort of poo is there? As a *connoisseur de crap* you will come to find that the variety is extraordinary. Lumpy, chunky, watery, smelly, totally odourless, compacted — and there's surprising ones too. Like regular dumps of what can only be pea and ham soup, even when baby has never eaten any. Or what about the 'roll away'? We haven't quite figured out what it is we feed him that creates these, but it's probably similar to the food airlines serve on long flights — the kind that binds you up. When the nappy gets opened, instead of the usual and predictable smear, there are hard little ball-like nuggets that have a habit of rolling away like ball bearings before you have a chance to catch them ... onto the floor, under the bed, under the furniture, behind the wardrobe ...

Then, of course, there's the 'unexpected' type of poo — because babies can take a dump whenever and wherever they feel relaxed enough to do so. For instance, picture yourself enjoying one of the great experiences of parenthood, the 'baby in the bath'.

Isn't baby cute? Big smile, having so much fun, covered in bubbles and splashing in the water. Isn't this what being a parent is all about? Look another big smile just for Daddy.

'Daddy loves you too,' you say and smile back. But hang on. Baby was sitting quiet for just a little too long ... and why was there that slight wincing? Oh my God! Insert the theme from *Jaws*.

Da-dum!

'What's that?'

Da-dum!

'In the water!'

Daaa-dum! Daaa-dum! Da, dum, dum, dum, dum, dum, dum!

'Aaaaghh!'

Now I'm going to go out on a limb here and guess, unless you're a plumber, you've never previously poked poo down a plughole before. To give you a warning — waterlogged poo is the smelliest, slipperiest, most difficult poo there is. It smears, it sticks and it stinks. So the big difficulty is how to rid yourself of it.

Firstly, bath time for baby must be immediately terminated and junior should be swung out before coming in contact with any bobbing, bubble-covered bog. You are now left with a bath full of bubbles and water and poo — poo that has a tendency to break up the longer it is left in the water, so you need to act fast.

Simply pulling out the plug and hoping it will neatly suck down the drain is just that: hope. It won't happen. What occurs is a long smear on the porcelain as it slides toward the plughole, the heavier pieces sticking to the bottom of the bath as the water runs out, while a mass of smaller bits sit in a small, smelly and sodden lump in the drain. This then requires poking, pushing and straining through the drain like a sieve.

Endeavouring *not* to come in contact with the poo — by reaching for some tissue paper to try and pick it out of the water — doesn't work either. Tissue paper and water simply don't mix. All you end up with is a flimsy pulp that practically dissolves around the poo on contact. Horrendous as this advice will sound: the quickest and easiest way to deal with this situation is by resorting to … yep … 'the scoop'.

Here's when a perspective check comes in. Have you ever watched those documentaries where people go back to the wild and have to survive on their basic hunting and gathering skills to keep themselves alive? Always been a little envious of the guy who can literally catch a fish in a shallow creek bed with his bare hands? It's not that hard, just a matter of practice ... and now here's your opportunity.

Stick your hand very gently into the bath water, trying not to create too many ripples that will break up the poop and, just like tickling the belly of a slumbering salmon, gently raise the poo from the water onto your palm and deposit it in the nearest toilet.

When I first realised I was *automatically* doing this I don't recall but, suffice to say, never in my wildest dreams did I believe I would one day find myself holding someone else's freshly laid do-do in the palm of my hand! Such are the 'joys' of parenthood. But wait ... there's more!

As uncomfortable and unsavoury as the thought may be (no, let me re-phrase that, as unsavoury as the thought is), you will, at some stage, find yourself routinely thrusting your nose into your child's pants and taking a good whiff. (That's right, just like dogs introducing themselves to each other. 'Oh hello! Is that Rex back there? Always good to catch up boy, but steady on! Curb the enthusiasm with that cold wet nose. You're beginning to moisten my prostate!')

Exactly when this became a relatively natural part of my life, one I rarely gave a second thought to, I don't remember. But, particularly when other people were around and we didn't want their nostrils assaulted, it wasn't long before my wife and I felt it necessary to ascertain as swiftly as possible whether our child had taken a dump in his jocks, or whether he was just passing a breeze through his pants. Unfortunately the only quick and easy way was to get up close and inhale a draft.

So as you can see, poo is something you are *expected* to come to terms with regardless of how 'emasculating' you may feel it is. How to do it and still maintain your masculine pride? The trick, as you've now seen, is ... PERSPECTIVE!

We men are task orientated, so turn nappy changing into a challenge! Think of those war movies where recruits with shaved heads and unnaturally sharp jaw lines are blindfolded and made to slam together disassembled rifles, all while a sadistic sergeant screams into their ears, fires a few shots from a Kalashnikov over their heads and times their efforts with a stopwatch. That's how to think of changing baby: a potentially life-saving combat skill that requires practice and precision because there will be times when it will feel just like that.

Example? After thirty-five years of loyal devotion to the hopeless jokes that I call my favourite football team, they somehow fluked their way into the Grand Final. Aware of the emotional fever pitch this event was stirring inside my proudly beating chest, my wife informed me that Grand Final day was the perfect day for a catch-up gossip with her girl-friends. Since I was planning to watch the game live on TV, I could also look after the baby!

Well, it wasn't ideal. The baby would need to be played with and fed and yes, *changed*. I wouldn't be able to become totally absorbed in every single moment of the match and I wouldn't be able to guzzle quite so much beer, but hey, I'd done it before and maybe baby would be happy being propped up in front of the TV. What better time to begin its induction as another proud supporter of Dad's favourite team? (Why I would want to inflict the curse of this pathetic team on my child I don't know, but I'm sure there's something in the Bible about children being made to pay for the sins of their fathers.)

Baby had other thoughts. It cried, it complained, it constantly dropped things it was playing with and needed them to be picked up and handed back ... and picked up and handed back ... and picked up and handed back ... and then it wanted to be burped and fed and changed. And then ... a miracle!

With the second half of the game about to begin he fell asleep. Yes! Baby's asleep, the wife is out, I am king of my castle and I'll be able to watch the second half of a game I've waited thirty-five years for — uninterrupted. It's a perfect afternoon in my new life as a father ... until ... the scores are tied. The teams are playing in extra time and it's been a colossal encounter. I'm jumping out of my chair. I'm yelling at the telly urging my team on, abusing them when they make errors and ringing my mates who are at a BBQ, drinking beer, laughing, belching and farting together in male camaraderie. Not that I mind too much, 'cause I'm a dad who's home alone and who's been so good as a father this day that my magnificent child is blissfully slumbering — warm, content and peaceful. Then, with only minutes to go, the scores are level and my team surging forward in attack — I smell something.

'It will pass,' I think to myself. 'Just gas.' Another nervous minute ticks by. The smell remains. The creature stirs. 'No, not now. Oh please not now ... sleep for just a little longer ... Please! ... ple ... '

'Waaaahhhh!!!!'

And it's not just any cry. It's the demanding, *must* be attended to immediately cry of, 'I have a full and stinky crappy between my legs that has to be changed and changed NOW!' Baby is not going to stop wailing till someone — there is only me — comes to help. This is where changing a nappy needs to be thought of as a life-saving combat skill.

This is when your training, ability and military efficiency comes into its own. Now is the moment that months of crappy changing has prepared you for! You need to attend to the baby! You need to get back in front of the telly! And soldier ... you need to do it fast!

Like so many things in life, practice and preparation are the key. Ensure that the change-table is clean and that within easy reach are some nappies *already* out of the packet. (For some reason flimsy plastic packaging that usually tears open in an instant at any ordinary, non-crucial moment will stretch and turn into something like vinyl whenever there is a need to be swift.)

Have the new nappy opened and ready to be tucked in under baby's butt as soon as the old one is pulled away. (A *disposable* nappy — if you're still looking for proof of its superiority over cloth — is much faster to use in a time-critical situation.) Similarly have a baby wipe (and why aren't they called 'bum wipes' because that's what they are!) open and extracted, ready to be used. Here you can even challenge yourself to guesstimate how many wipes each change will require. With experience you will come to know simply from the weight and the smell of the nappy.

Remember, you'll be working with only one hand here (sometimes in the dark), because the other hand will be holding two squirming, pulling and struggling legs. Roll the old nappy upon itself, securing the contents within, shoot for the basket (the nearest bin), grab baby and sprint back to the TV.

Trust me, you will have to master this skill otherwise your life will become one long and unsatisfying *sportus interruptus*! And, like I said earlier, it's not only what comes out of baby's rear, there's the other end as well. Oh, yes! *Vomit* has come to be a very big talking point in our household also. Poo *and* vomit! We're thrilling people to be around. No wonder we never see our non-parent friends any more.

If you have ever been to the home of someone with a newborn you may have noticed how 'untidy' their home has suddenly become. Sure, you're not a complete philistine — you realise that it must be a little more difficult to maintain a *Vogue* home now that there's a baby in the house. But these people have really let themselves go! You notice the little white towels, boxes of tissues, rolls of absorbent paper towelettes and baby wipes all over the place: on coffee tables, hanging off the back of chairs, stuffed inside magazine racks, next to stereos, on top of lamp shades, in fact — all over the house. Why aren't the towels folded and in the bathroom, the baby room or in a linen cupboard somewhere? Why aren't the tissues and paper towels discreetly hidden in a cupboard? What has happened to their house pride?

What's happened is this: while you see haphazard sloppiness, parents see strategic positioning because babies have the unsettling habit of vomiting. Unexpectedly. Without warning. At any moment. In any place. And for no particular reason, so you need, literally within arm's reach, something to quickly wipe it up, no matter what part of the house you're in.

And vomit gets the same in-depth discussion and analysis as the other stuff. Colour, amount, texture, viscosity, volume and, when baby is shooting for distance, the area covered! All of this now takes on an incredible importance. Where once we seriously discussed the merits of a fine wine, we now mull and muse over the content of our son's pants or what's gone hurtling from his mouth onto the carpet, while closely inspecting some chunks caught in mum's hair on the way.

But why stop there?

'You mean there's more?' I hear you say with horror and incredulity. 'We're talking babies. Nice little pudgy things with happy faces? Tell me you're making all this up?'

Well I'm not. I'm just trying to warn you. Not only is there poo and vomit — but when the baby is sick or has a cold (some kids get eight a year!) — there's mucus. Mucus by the bucket-load! Thick great slimy lengths of glossy wet gelatinous tendrils. Gloopy snot that trails from nostril to chin, then gets smeared across the face, wrists, hands and sleeves, ending up caked dry in hair, eyelids and any other body part a hand can reach.

Why? Because babies can't 'blow' (I'd call this a design fault ... but more on that later). You therefore need to remove this gloop for them and to do this properly requires practice and precision. You can't just take a casual swipe at the stuff because it has the ability to retract and reduce itself. It's like trying to pick up mercury, it simply oozes away from the point of contact. To catch a thread you need to pincer it between thumb and forefinger and pull it out by the roots. To achieve this requires you to grip the offending substance firmly but not too hard, otherwise it simply squeezes out the sides of your fingers or snaps off short, and you then have to go back and try again, usually as your suffering child pulls and tugs and bites and fights to get away from you.

Strangely enough, you just might find that it is at precisely these sort of times when parenthood, at its absolute worst, is also at its absolute best.

Imagine you're into your sixth month of unrelenting, sleep deprived exhaustion. It's 3 a.m. and you've already been up several times checking and nursing a sick baby. You have a crucial breakfast business meeting first thing that morning, it's the busiest week your company has ever faced and it's only Tuesday.

In the dark you're grappling to hold the baby in one hand, while with the other correctly draw out a dosage of insanely priced, red-coloured baby medicine from a tiny eye dropper so small you can't read the measurement, before attempting to squirt it down the gullet of the exhausted, wailing baby with the raw sore throat. Even though you hold its head in a vice-like grip (and hate yourself for having to be so brutal), the baby still manages to flay at you with arms and legs, squirming and contorting its body and getting a few lucky kicks in on your nose, eyes and, of course, your groin. You are both smeared with mucus, and from its painful, hacking cough, the red-dyed medicine, spittle and dribble flies through the air (along with bits of last night's dinner).

It's right then ... that the little arms flop over your shoulder, its worn out body falls against you, snuggles up close and you feel the warm, wet, sticky sensation of thick mucus and drool being smeared along your neck. As baby falls asleep in your arms, you hold on tight and wonder at the depth of love you can never explain to someone who isn't a parent.

You summon up some reserves of energy, rock softly back and forth and then gently, reluctantly place the slumbering babe into its cot. You take a long, lingering look at the angel you've helped to create and as you quietly tiptoe out of the room ... the little bastard starts screaming again! At this point your neurons literally congeal. You inform the child's mother it's *her turn* and you go outside to curl up in the kennel with the dogs.

I TRY TO SEE IT NOT AS A DESIGN FAULT, BUT MORE AS GOD HAVING A SENSE OF HUMOUR.
GOLDING

Chapter 9

Design Fault #1 — Falling Over

Many men understand that the problems fathers face could be overcome if the mother did her job properly and gestation lasted a little longer — like about three years longer! It's quite obvious, with only the most cursory glance at a couple of David Attenborough docos, that we as a species are simply not 'cooked' long enough. This is a biological design fault.

Animals with brains the size of pinheads are able to get up and move around and fend for themselves right from birth. Long, wobbly legged things like horses and wildebeests can get up and run along with mum in less time than it takes to lick up the afterbirth. (Mmm, some things *are* better left to nature!) Not we humans.

The more I watch my gorgeous child the more

I'm amazed that we, as a species, managed to survive at all. Not only is there a design fault in the gestation period, which is probably only a third as long as it should be, but the baby itself is configured all wrong.

The arms and legs are too short; the muscles are underdeveloped. It can't control its own body temperature and it's got no fur to keep it warm. Worst of all it's got this enormous head — a melon that just keeps expanding while the rest of the body tries to catch up. In fact, by its first birthday, a baby's brain is already three quarters the size of a fully-grown adult's.

As time passes, baby starts to take control of the machine it's in and after months of frustrated crawling, finally masters the ability to stand up and take its first steps. Now baby has not only to maintain balance and move forward on just two legs (while most other animals have four) but it has to do it with a huge lump of bone and a wobbly brain that are way up above its centre of gravity.

Strangely enough it falls over a lot ... more often than not whacking its enormous Elephant Man noggin when it hits the deck! Ow! Obviously, this is a design fault and baby should be returned to the manufacturer.

Look at the other animals. They're not falling

around on the ground 'cause their heads are too big and heavy to hold up. Baby elephants don't suddenly teeter over and sprawl about with their legs kicking in the air. Calves don't keep dropping onto their big wet noses bleating to be picked up. The real impetus for homo erectus to leave the safety of the forest canopy was probably because falling on your head from the treetops was just too painful.

Funny thing is, smart as grown-ups are, it's only been in relatively recent years that anyone has bothered to take a child's perspective of life into consideration. It's only been a short time since laws have been introduced to make playgrounds and schoolyards safe for our kids and their colossal craniums.

As a kid my school play areas were covered with asphalt — that's the stuff they build highways out of, for crying out loud! So as little kids we not only had to contend with the unstoppable urge to constantly run around like freaks hyped-up on speed because of all the sugar in our food and drinks, but the more we ran the higher the incidence of tripping over and, of course, that meant landing on … that's right … asphalt!

'Bitumen! That'll keep the school ground maintenance costs down,' some insensitive bureaucrat probably proposed to some equally thick and thoughtless departmental head of some non-caring government agency!

I don't think a day would have gone by when there wasn't a kid bleeding from some part of its body. If not the head, then certainly from skinned knees and shredded palms. Sometimes you'd manage to put your hands out in front to save your chin from whacking into the road surface of the 'playground' only to end up with gravel rash imbedded under the skin for a week! And to think we look back at the Victorian era of Dickens and imagine times were harsh for children. At least they had mud to break their falls.

Chapter 10

Design Fault #2 — Discipline

One of the main reasons fathers struggle with babies is because they're so damn disorderly. They will simply not do what they're told. This is not the neat and disciplined world we men are used to. This is not, 'Sir! Yes, sir! How high was that again, sir?'

Not only is a baby a cumbersome, unresponsive thing but it forces us to stretch our vocabulary and communication skills. For simple creatures such as we men, who get by with conversations of barely more than extended grunts — Wanna drink beer? Wanna watch footy? Wanna hide the sausage? — this is a problem.

It means men must learn to think through issues, and this is something most of us have studiously avoided all our lives. Working out problems in the abstract we're good at. Quantum physics? No

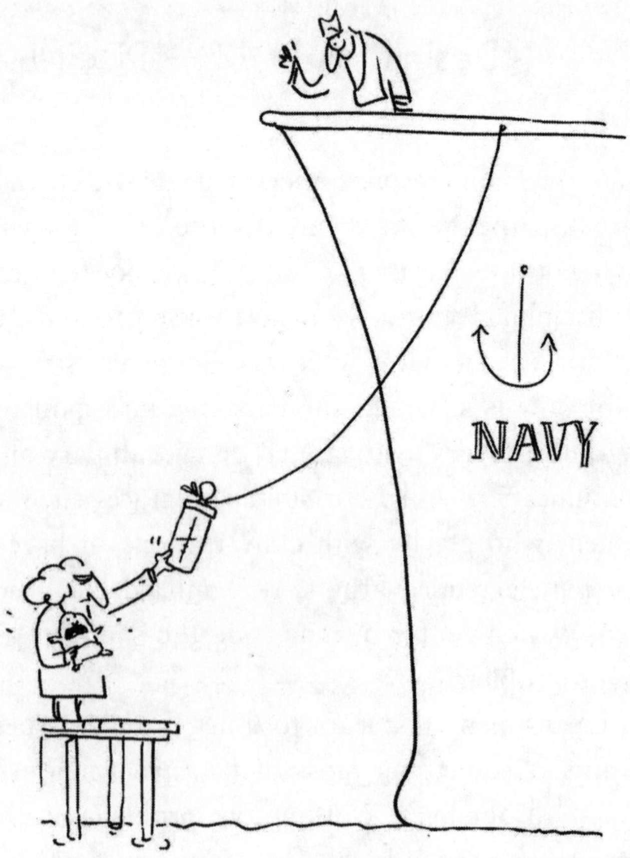
NAVY

problem. Load bearings, logarithms — horse racing? Easy.

A baby, however, forces us to think differently, to try to consider the world from someone else's viewpoint, from someone else's needs and emotions. All of a sudden so much more is demanded of us. Why?

We haven't changed. We're still the same loveable guys we always were. The same guys who don't have enough sense to realise that at 4 a.m. with a skin full of booze another round of tequila slammers and beer chasers is *not* such a great idea ... no matter how many times we make the same mistake. And it's not as if fathers don't try: 'Wanna dummy?', 'Wanna change your nappy?', 'Wanna eat?'

No response? It's not our fault baby is delivered into the world by mum a little underdone!

This then is the real reason why men invented the navy. If there were no wars to fight and no enemy to engage, men would still have invented the navy, because men like to go to sea for extended periods of time for one very good reason: babies.

After a tour of duty of a few years, when the man returns home, if their wife or partner has done the right thing, the now three- or four-year-old child should know its name, have a fair idea of right and wrong, will understand discipline and order, and may even be able to kick a ball. Now we've got something that a man can work with!

Remember the scene from *The Sound of Music* where the father, an Austrian naval commander (isn't Austria landlocked?), comes home and his seven children line up in descending order of age and size? At the command from a whistle they each smartly march forward, state their names, stamp their feet and then return to their place, standing rigidly to attention. Have you ever noticed the difference in men and women watching this? The women look outraged and shocked. The men, however ... Well, we know we're supposed to be outraged and shocked but really, deep down, men love this part of what, after all, is a mind-numbingly long, saccharine sweet, frilly, girly movie. If only all children could be that well trained the world would be a simpler and more pleasant place. And who wouldn't love kids?

'Hello Father. It's a pleasure to meet you, sir. May I play quietly outside while you sit and watch sport on the TV and Mother prepares you a drink and your evening meal?'

Men's whole attitude to children would be different. 'What's that? You're pregnant again. Wow, that's terrific news. No problem. Gee, I hope it's twins. Kids are great.'

Chapter 11

Design fault #3 — Soft Spots

If the previous points do not convince you that women are not doing their part when it comes to babies — that they are in fact wimping out and giving birth at least a couple of years sooner than they should — then here's more to prove that the human baby is just about the least matured of any species at birth.

New babies have a 'soft spot' on the top of their heads. Some have two! This spot, the 'fontanelle', is a bit of skin and membrane that conveniently covers an area where there is no bone and so stops their brains falling out at inopportune moments. The membrane is there because the baby's skull hasn't 'fused' together properly. An obvious design fault — but there's more.

Baby's soft, under-developed head also requires

HONEY, THE CHILD'S BEEN RECALLED...THEY'VE FOUND A FEW DESIGN FAULTS!
GOLDING

regular rotation! That's not to say you need to get all Linda Blair (the actress from *The Exorcist*) with it, but baby's head needs to be frequently turned to ensure that it doesn't develop 'flat' planes in its shape from being left with its ginormous skull in the one place for too long. That's right, just like a lump of wet clay slowly spreading on a potter's wheel.

In addition, when putting bub down for a sleep you must pay attention to tucking the ears flat under its head. If you do not pay close attention to this, baby's ears will grow straight out, giving it the appearance of a wing nut ... or royalty!

So, not only can human babies not get up quickly after birth and run with the rest of the herd, it actually takes a few months for their heads to 'harden' properly. What more need be said to support the theory that, like urns in a kiln, women simply don't keep their buns in the oven long enough?

GOLDING

Chapter 12

Helping Out #1 — Cleaning

OK, here's some tough stuff to accept that no one warned me about when I was a pre-parent male. As a bloke you won't like what I'm going to say, but it needs to be stated and you should be prepared. As the 'bloom' of your partner's pregnancy continues to blossom (you'll learn the term 'bloated' is rarely appreciated!), you will be required to 'help out around the house'.

Odious as the thought may be, you might even find that you are expected to continue 'helping out' *after* the child is born! For some men, there's even the mind-numbing consequence that after the birth you may be required (are you sitting down for this?) to 'help out' for the rest of time!

Yes, that's right! ...'women's work'! Shocking

and incomprehensible I know, but at least you've been warned. Oh, and saying, 'But I already take the garbage out' may find you reposing on the lounge for an extended period of time.

The thing is, we blokes look down on 'women's work', 'house work' and 'domestic duties' because it all seems pretty low-grade. It's not building something. It's not creating something. It's not clinching a deal!

It seems boring and dull — monotonous, mundane and repetitious, but it needs to be done because it's important. Not only do you want a clean home to live and entertain in, but you need a hygienic environment for the baby.

The difficult thing is, in today's society, it's hard for us blokes to assert the necessary moral high ground that has allowed men for the past 50,000 years to get out of doing it. I've tried to argue with The Boss that, 'Men don't do this stuff.' But with razor sharp intuition she cuts me down, delivering a precisely crafted, 'Why not?'

Has this woman trained with the United Nations? Where has she learnt so skilfully to manipulate the language and turn the content of my argument on its head for all the hollow and empty rhetoric it is? I'm left floundering. Stumbling and fumbling for an equally swift and succinct reply, only to find her looking at me with that, 'What a pathetic excuse for a man I've married' expression, when the best I can come up with is a flaccid, ''Cause we don't?'

You see, the whole concept of women's work is now somewhat irrelevant. Sure, when men were 'hunters' and women were 'gatherers' the menial tasks naturally fell to the ones who weren't out there each day risking life and limb, being mauled by mammoths and wrestling with rhinos. Plus, physically, who was going to argue with the set-up? The brute with the brawn was in charge and the women simply fitted in.

Even relatively recently, when most men worked really hard (actually sweating and straining physically!), there was some general reason for women to do the 'domestic' duties. It was a fair trade off. These days though ... gee I don't know. A lot of guys might be putting in the hours, but with the technology and communication revolution a lot of blokes aren't exactly 'straining' any more.

Sitting behind a desk, tapping into a computer and doing deals via the Internet isn't quite the same as a five-day chase through the jungle running down a mastodon. Even 'traditional' male jobs aren't as irksome as they used to be — like driving a truck. It may involve long hours and it may be *aggravating*, particularly if you're in city traffic, but with air conditioning, power steering, CD players, CB radios, ergonomic, pneumatically adjustable seating, tinted windows, well ... it's not quite the hot, hard, dusty work it used to be.

In fact, as technology, communications and machinery improve, as more physical effort is taken out of work — the more 'maternal' society becomes — the more irrelevant we drones are becoming. What's the point of being the stronger sex when so many things can now be done just as easily by the fairer sex?

Don't get me wrong, I know a lot of blokes work a lot of long hours and there are some trades that are still physically demanding, but you've got to admit there's plenty of 'men's jobs' that aren't all that tough. Yet we still try to get out of the 'housework' because we know it's thankless and about as joyful as digging a trench and filling it in again. Every day.

This is where I struggle to find the moral high ground that once was simply a given. ('I was born a male, therefore I don't have to do this stuff, damn it!') It's hard to justify putting something down as 'menial' and 'lowly' when it's probably more physically demanding and important to the health of your family than anything else you do.

So how can men deal with this world where they

should do more of the baby and house stuff, while retaining a sense of masculine pride and independence? Really it's not that hard to do. Once again, it's simply a matter of perspective.

You need to begin looking at domestic chores as if you were entering a dangerous, unpredictable and wild environment, or better still, a battlefield ... because that's what it's like! It's you against the elements. Take ironing for instance.

When most men think of ironing they think of 'girly' stuff. They see little wobbly ironing boards and piles of clothes that need creases 'just so'. They see dainty, frilly collars and clothes made of silk, satin and weird stretchy materials. Not me!

When I see an iron I see a shiny, super heated, heavy piece of metal that shoots hot jets of scalding steam! I see control settings and little openings into which you have to constantly pour water to maintain the broiling clouds that emanate from the searing metal. When I see an iron, I see a long cable hanging out of a dangerous piece of machinery, plugged into an electric power socket. In short, when I see an iron, I don't see an appliance ... I see a *tool*! And I know I not only have to work closely with this tool but I have to become intimate with it. It has to be dominated and mastered.

With fire extinguisher at the ready and while

wearing elbow-length asbestos gloves it must be firmly and forcefully grabbed by the handle and constantly grappled with to maintain control. You have to ensure fingers are not run over by the scalding hot base, that skin is not shot with blistering steam and that toes cannot be crushed if the heavy metal weight is accidentally dropped. Meanwhile, you have to tug, pull and manoeuvre the piece of attire, ensuring you do not scorch the material or set the board ablaze.

What about vacuuming? Again ... perspective. You should look upon a vacuum cleaner as a large, loud industrial tool, like a jackhammer, an air compressor or a generator. You wouldn't just walk up to one and kick it into action would you? No ... you'd prepare!

Firstly, you should have to undergo a graduate course in domestic science that leaves you with a certificate or diploma, something that says you are capable of adjusting nozzle lengths, fitting the correct attachment for the particular surface or nook to be vacuumed and that you understand the 'suck setting'. The suck setting is the certain amount or quotient of 'suck' required for a particular purpose. This is something you need to know. Most blokes set a vacuum cleaner to 'full suck' and just start vacuuming away. As I found out from the torn and shredded material left hanging in front of our windows, this is not the most appropriate setting for going over lace curtains!

To avoid premature deafness from vacuuming, it is only sensible to take the same precautions you would in any noisy industrial situation. Therefore don a pair of big plastic earmuffs — the kind that are bright orange or yellow and worn in factories or building sites. Pressure bandages for your elbows and shoulders are also recommended to protect against the repetitive strain of pushing the nozzle back and forth, back and forth, back and forth. Plus, it's essential to wear a weight belt, as proper vacuuming involves a lot of lifting, shifting and moving of furniture.

Then there's dealing with what's under the bookcase, the sideboard, the lounge suite. That's right … dead things! Horrible, nasty, creepy, fluttery things. Cockroaches! Moths! Spiders! Millipedes! Women don't want to know about that stuff. Dealing with dead things, rotting corpses, is what men do, by God! (By the way, you'll do a lot more killing when baby comes along because, unless it's got a wet nose and a wagging tail, The Boss sees anything with more than two legs as a potential threat — which brings me to the point of karma. How come women want them dead but men have to do the killing?

Does this mean in the next life women advance to a higher place while we come back as dung beetles?)

To assist with your transition in perspective, put these damn tools where they belong. Appliances live in cupboards and closets — *tools* live in a shed! So get them out there in your shed or garage where the heavy, greasy things are kept. And if you're one of those anal types (or in language that makes people feel better about their defects — an 'A' type personality), and you have outline diagrams where each individual tool hangs in its own little space, then get the heavy felt pen and draw around the vacuum cleaner, the iron and the ironing board, bend a couple of nails and proudly hang the new additions to your tool set alongside the wrenches, pliers, drills, hammers and saws.

Still need convincing that telling battle tales about the house cleaning over a beer with your mates can't be as dramatic as the D-Day landings or pouring molten steel at a smelter? Does dusting, cleaning and polishing still sound a bit 'nancy' to you? Don't you believe it!

It's a fact that exposure to pollution inside a house is up to fifteen times higher than outside. Thick rubber gloves, a face mask and protective eyeglasses are the bare essentials for cleaning bathrooms, kitchens and surfaces. Full-face oxygen breathing apparatus is preferable but most households can't quite stretch to this, though, like smoke alarms and a small fire extinguisher, they should. Have you seen the ingredients in these products? This is nothing short of chemical warfare!

Talk about weapons of mass destruction. Teams of UN chemical weapons inspectors should be sent into the cupboards under a kitchen sink! Here's what's on the labels of just some of the cans and bottles of everyday, run-of-the-mill cleaning products: solvents; anionic and non-anionic surfactants; sodium hypochlorite; sodium hydroxide; chlorine; alkalines; denatured alcohol; ethyl alcohol; benzalkonium; and ethanolamine. How about this: disodium cocoamphodiacetate and … I swear this is not a made up word — well not made up by me at any rate — methylchloroisothiazolinone! Words I can hardly spell let alone pronounce!

If that's not enough, they all have warnings such as: 'Flammable liquid'; 'Corrosive'; 'Do not get on clothes'; 'Avoid contact with eyes and skin'; 'If swallowed induce vomiting'; 'Do not induce vomiting'; 'Contact your doctor or local poisons information centre immediately'; and 'Do not spray near electrical connections or switches'!

Not only that but when dusting and polishing, most people will close windows and doors to avoid having the mess simply blow to another spot around the house. This effectively concentrates exposure to these chemicals and their noxious vapours, the very same products with warnings saying 'ensure adequate ventilation'!

So who do you think now tells my wife off when she goes near the cupboard doors or the shiny clean fridge and leaves smear marks? Me, that's who! You know why? Because it's damned aggravating when you've scrubbed something clean to have someone carelessly start crapping it up again! Trust me. Try it.

So there you go! I told you it might be difficult to hear but at least you've been warned. Flick the perspective switch from boring, repetitive, low-grade 'domestic' duty to important and potentially dangerous, and housework can become not only a breeze but a thoroughly competitive challenge!

Chapter 13

Helping Out #2 — Shopping

As part of 'helping out' you may find yourself required to assist with the shopping as well as the cleaning. If you haven't ventured into a supermarket for a while, then you may be in for a surprise. Things have changed in the last few years and there've been some real advances in variety — even in products you didn't imagine could be diversified.

The intricacies of supermarkets begin to be especially important to prospective fathers when the cravings of pregnant women come into play. My wife's cravings were for 'Blue Lizards' — crushed-ice drink things, drizzled with blue-coloured flavouring — and tuna! (Not together, although from what I'm told, it would not be an unusual combination for some mums-to-be.)

As the pregnancy wore on it became more

7 ITEMS OR LESS
7 BABIES OR LESS
BEER
GOLDING

physically difficult for my wife to get out and about (coupled with a fear of her water 'breaking', whatever that is, in such a public place). The time came when I was handed a list and sent to 'help out' with the shopping. Among other things on the list my darling princess had written 'tuna'.

The last time I bought a can of tuna, the only choice was size. I either bought the big can, the medium can or the fiddly little ring-pull can that was hardly worth the effort involved in opening it. If I wanted variety, I bought salmon.

What I was totally unprepared for was the choice now available for the lowly tuna. I stood bedazzled in front of a section of supermarket that stretched away into the distance with cans upon cans of tuna in all kinds of variety. Tuna in brine; tuna in springwater; tuna in aspic; tuna with lemon and cracked pepper; with capsicum and roman tomatoes; with zesty vinaigrette, lemongrass, lime, curry, ginger, spices ... a never-ending kaleidoscope of variety and flavour. I was fully expecting to find tuna in asses' milk, lightly sauteed with onions, garlic and served on a bed of wild rice ... in a can!

I mean, it's good to have choices in life but, with some things, too much choice is just, well ... *too much*. But remember about being supportive? Fearful of the terrible hormonal abuse I would receive if I came home with the wrong tuna, I stumbled out of the aisle wheeling a trolley overflowing with one of each variety, unsure as to which tuna my wife was referring. Turning into another aisle I proceeded to find the next item on the shopping list.

Have you tried to buy a toothbrush lately?! It used to be that a brush was a brush and they all did the job. Now though ... Different colours; different sizes; different designs. Bits that bend; bits that narrow; bits that curve. Handles with rubber grips; handles with contours; handles with sparkles. Bristles that point in thirty different directions; bristles that lose colour as they age; bristles that are soft, medium, hard and semi-permeable.

Then there are the electric ones that cost so much I don't even bother putting them in the equation! Who in their right mind pays that much money for something you place in your mouth and slobber all over? I mean really, how hard is it to push your own brush?

On top of all this, the manufacturers are so into 'added value', that when you do find a brush you like, the next time you go shopping that model has been superseded and is no longer in stock, so you have to start choosing all over again, trying to guess which one will best serve your needs.

You know, we're only allocated so much time on

this world and I could feel the life oozing from me as I stood in that crowded supermarket aisle pushed and buffeted by those around me, staring at the toothbrush section mesmerised (and a little addle-pated), while dreary and distorted music scratched out of a crackly speaker.

'Mop and bucket to aisle two where ten years of a man's life has seeped out onto the floor.'

What do you do? How do you choose? The only way through it for me was to act like a man. I methodically started to categorise and make comparisons!

The medium bristle, micro head, with sparkle handle for $3.95.

The soft outer bristle, medium inner bristle, diamond shaped head with non slip rubber grip contour handle for $4.10.

The polygon shaped head with soft concave outer bristles, rounded on the ends, combined with forty-five-degree-angled polyurethane epoxy acetate hard inner bristles, geometrically arranged in concentric circles of diminishing length, arranged along the Le Corbusier influenced, Italian-designed handle with non-slip nodules, each hand carved and individually numbered in a stylised pattern that echoes the rhythmic perfection of the Parthenon, plus built-in alarm clock and compass that emits the soothing sounds of whales mating for $4.95.

Well, with all that going for it, it has to be the $4.95 brush. Right? Wrong! Why? Because there is another level of complexity. This magnificent brush only comes in red and I now know (from painful and humiliating experience) red doesn't *work* in our bathroom.

This is the kind of thing my wife knows about instinctively. She knows immediately what will and won't *colour coordinate*. What will or won't match with the towels. What will or won't clash with the tiles and what will or won't *flare* against the colourful little perfume soaps no one ever uses. That's right, not only is the variety of features bewildering to the point of nausea, there's the added pressure to bring home one that matches the decor, even, and I must stress this, if your brushes get hidden away inside a cabinet!

This, of course, is something I can't do, something of which I have no concept of, simply because I am a male. A straight male to be precise — which reminds me I can't dance either, but that's a whole different subject.

I mean really, how did life for men become so complicated? Here we are: normal cost-conscious males unable even to make the simple purchase of a toothbrush ... and I haven't even started on the toothpaste, mouthwash and floss!

You know what settled the dilemma? I didn't buy a brush in the supermarket because I was booked in for a dental check up the next day and he 'recommended' I should use one of the expensive electric toothbrushes. And you know what? With my mouth full of another man's hands; sharp metal objects scraping at my teeth; water, spittle and smoke (where did that come from?) flying out of my mouth; and despite my reluctance ever to pay so much money for something so utilitarian, I gladly handed over the cash. That's right, I happily parted with nearly twice the amount of money for the very same toothbrush I'd dismissed in the supermarket! Why?

For the sheer relief of having someone else make the decision for me. Someone authoritative. Someone even my wife couldn't argue with.

'Sorry darling. I understand the colour is all wrong for our bathroom decor but what could I say? The dentist recommended it. And anyway, with cartoon characters and musical chimes, it makes me want to brush!'

So the next day I get handed a new shopping list and this time I have to buy toilet paper. Now I know it's good to have choices in life but have you tried to buy toilet paper lately … ?

I'VE GOT SOME NEWS...
IT MIGHT BE BEST
IF YOU SIT!
I'VE GOT SOME NEWS...
IT MIGHT BE BEST
IF YOU SIT
GOLDING

Chapter 14

Patterning

If you've watched enough documentaries you'll be familiar with the term 'patterning'. For example, the first thing a newly hatched chicken sees is 'Mummy' and will therefore follow 'Mummy' around, whether it happens to be a chicken, a lovable dog or an annoying kid.

In human terms, however, patterning is nothing to do with the child latching onto the parent; it's the other way around. Parents 'pattern' onto their child, usually calling it 'bonding', when in most cases it's outright obsession.

You see, to be honest, few newborns really give a stuff who's feeding them, wiping their butts or tucking them into the cot. As long as it's done they're happy. What occurs in the parent brain, however, is something quite extraordinary.

When my wife and I were pre-parents, we had our dogs and we loved them. When we went for walks, people would stop us in the street and ask about our dogs. They would say, 'Aren't they adorable', 'What breed are they?', 'What a nice coat', 'Do they always do that to people's legs?' Stuff like that.

We would smile and chat and allow their children to pat the dogs. They were a part of our little family and we basked in the glow of people's affection for our 'kids'.

As I've already mentioned, I can honestly say I never noticed whether anyone was out on the street with a baby or not. I always smiled and chatted to other people walking their dogs but I don't ever recall people with prams.

Now of course it's different. Babies and their parents are suddenly everywhere. We peer at each other's babies in passing and smile knowingly, sharing a silent camaraderie, experiences of sleepless nights, endless nappy changes and feeling as if we'll never see our friends, go to a movie or out to dinner ever again.

The other thing that's changed is dogs just don't seem quite as interesting as they once did. Not only that but I expect everyone else in the world to be similarly dumbstruck by the magnificence of our baby as we are. I expect the same kinds of admiring looks, smiles and spontaneously open and freely given remarks and compliments about our baby as we used to receive for our dogs but it doesn't happen. Now, if we are out walking our baby and the dogs, most people passing still make all the right noises about our dogs but only a few of them, usually other new parents, make mention of our baby!

Why not? What's wrong with these people? Can't they see he is, in all likelihood, the most perfect specimen of human babyness ever created? Don't they know they're in the presence of a near perfect child, a child who at one point we believed, in all seriousness, might have been the reincarnation of the next Dalai Lama? Seriously!

We believed that one day I would head off to work, open the front door and there would be 5000 cross-legged, saffron robed, chanting monks (AND Richard Gere ... my wife particularly used to mention that point), paying homage to our child. (Hey, it has to happen to someone, right?)

Why don't other people publicly fall all over themselves, gushing with platitudes and compliments just as our baby's parents and grandparents do? It's because we've been 'patterned' to see our baby that way and they haven't.

Learned types have actually done studies that show we as a species are hard wired to go all soft and mushy whenever we see something that looks like a baby — that is, something with big eyes and a head out of all proportion to its body. A baby's head, as I've mentioned, is oversized — in fact it is twice the size of an adult head when compared to the body. What other animal looks like this? For one thing, the koala. According to the studies, if you took away the round fuzzy ears and gave it a pointy snout people would see the animal for the scratching, biting, flea infested beastie it is. No more getting up close to have a cuddle with what looks like a tree-climbing rat. What about the panda bear? Again give it pointy ears, remove the big black patches of fur on its face so all you can see are its little piggy eyes and all of a sudden — 'Hello extinction!' — because nobody's going to be donating money to keep *that* alive.

Yet I can't help feeling a little sorry for our dogs; to tell the truth, I feel terrible. The dogs used to be our kids. We picked them out in a litter when they were only a couple of days old and looked like little guinea pigs suckling away with their eyes shut tight; brother and sister beagles to keep each other company.

Yeah, I know. I can hear you saying, 'Ohh. That's so sweet! Just like Snoopy.'

(You are someone who hasn't owned a 'Snoopy'. If you *have* had beagles you will instead be shaking your head from side to side in sympathy. It was no mere fluke that Charles M. Schulz chose a beagle for his eccentric, self-centred yet disarmingly charming cartoon dog.)

Anyway, we brought them home in a basket full of warm blankets and gave them puppy food and nutrients. I used to come home at lunchtime to feed them and check on them, and when they destroyed our shoes and peed on the carpet we smiled and thought them cute and we loved them dearly. They would wander around the house, sleep on the lounge and we'd let them in on weekend mornings to jump on our bed. We'd even go for drives and long walks down the beach and in parks.

In fact, we used to joke to people that we had brought them to 'practise with' and that after managing to keep them alive and relatively healthy for a few years then maybe we would be responsible enough to have a 'real' baby! For the beagles, that was their downfall; the beginning of the end.

As the pregnancy progressed, interest in 'our kids' declined dramatically. The long walks and adventures in the car fell away and they found themselves spending a lot more time outside, particularly as my wife starting doing that nesting thing toward the end of the pregnancy. She would tidy and fuss constantly so that the house would be just right — neat and efficiently operational when she and the baby came home, knowing full well that if it was left to me the place would look like a construction site.

The dogs probably started to pick up on the change when they were suddenly told areas of the house and things in it, like baby's room and fluffy teddy bears, were off limits. Not in a nice way either — they were yelled at and chased out and had fingers waggled at them.

If there was any doubt that something ominous was happening they worked it out the day I came home with one of the first of our baby's nappies and vigorously rubbed it into their soft furry faces. This, I'd been told, was a good way for dog owners to ensure that their pets quickly understood that they were about to be pushed down the pecking order. Now, of course, sniffing at 'poop' is usually a pretty interesting and entertaining thing for dogs. This was different though.

Once spoiled, loved and cherished above all else, our 'babies' were now 'the dogs'. 'Dad' was now 'master' and their lives were never to be the same. That said, if you do have dogs and find a similar situation unfolding, and you feel bad about the dog's demotion, check your perspective and remember this: dogs are resilient. They are adaptive and opportunistic. While you might have difficulty suppressing nausea the first time baby hurls a chunky pile onto the floor, you'll usually find your dog whips in past your legs to dive nose deep in this stinking, steamy, curdled porridge ... and loves you for it!

GOLDING

Chapter 15

Exercise — The Baby Workout

For a lot of parents, the advent of a new baby presents quite a disruption to the normal routine. Sleep, work, social life, going out, staying up late, nursing a hangover — everything normal gets thrown into turmoil as the family tries to adjust to the responsibility of baby's constant need for feeding, burping, changing, comfort and attention (all the things that used to be the sole domain of you, the man of the house!).

This can mean that regular exercise becomes difficult. For new fathers, simply finding the time can be difficult and even if you do manage to grab a free hour you can sometimes feel a pang of conscience that perhaps you should be doing something to 'help out', or you're probably so sleep deprived that the thought of exercise is too overwhelming to contemplate. Let's face it, it's hard to maintain muscle tone and aerobic fitness when you fall asleep between getting up off the lounge and walking to open the front door!

If you're the type of guy that swims or jogs or goes to the gym regularly this can be annoying and frustrating. Those Charles Atlas abs and Bullworker biceps can really drop away fast. And if you are the sedentary type, don't think that you get off the hook. If you're at the other end of the scale — where the idea of a workout is leaning forward to pick up the remote — you're in for a painful shock. Having a baby around the house necessitates effort. You will quickly feel muscles in all sorts of places you never knew you had because babies require a lot of picking up and putting down.

The trick once again ... is perspective! Simply start to think of baby time as exercise time! The great thing about combining the two is that it not only allows you the excuse of playing with baby and getting a great work out, but it lets you work up a number of baby *bonus* points.

Remember how you've had that uneasy feeling ever since the announcement that your wife or partner has been secretly assessing your quality and worth as a father? Well, the truth is, *she has*. And this scrutiny has also been coming from close relatives too. That's why being seen to play with your baby, wanting to, even, means points in your favour. You will be talked about as a 'wonderful' father for picking up junior in what appears your desire to have some playtime, when in fact you're secretly using bub as a static weight. Here are a few simple routines:

When placing junior in or out of the 'playpen' (a 'cage' for any other animal), don't do it just once, do it a few times. With back upright, slowly bend at the knees and then straighten up again. Feel those thighs burning! Your baby will like the sensation of being lifted up and down and may reward you with a smile or giggle ... baby bonus points will be credited to your account by any relative who may be watching.

If your baby throws its dummy onto the floor as you are carrying it from one room to another, don't quickly bend down and pick it up! Instead, position yourself just behind the dummy, feet pointing straight ahead with a shoulder-width stance. Then, holding your baby in front of you (but close to your body so there is no undue strain on your lower back), slowly squat down, taking a deep breath in as you descend and allow your baby to grab the dummy. Then slowly rise up again breathing out as you go. This will work the quads while assisting your baby's development of fine motor skills and finger coordination. Good for you; good for baby!

For shoulders and pecs try this:

Holding your baby out in front, facing you, feet

shoulder width, arms straight, simply raise and lower your kid. For a variation, lie on your back, knees up with the soles of the feet firmly on the ground and with your baby sitting on your chest. Now grab bub and lift up and down in the air, slowly bringing junior back down onto your chest. This will tone your shoulders and chest and should produce a big smile and a fit of giggles from your baby. Again that means if there's an audience you are gaining a major number of 'what a great dad' points.

If you're looking to define the 'sixpack gut', then sit ups — using your baby in place of a medicine ball — are effective. (Although it is probably best not to use your baby in a paired situation, throwing it back and forth between you and your workout partner. Leave that kind of skill to visiting Chinese acrobatic groups!)

Stand with your feet shoulder-width apart and your baby curled up safely under one arm. Then bend sideways at the waist and use your stomach muscles to straighten up again. Repeat the reps with your baby under the other arm.

And here's the real beauty of the baby workout: as your strength and flexibility is increasing, junior is gaining weight. So just when you feel the need to add extra kilos to your workout, baby does it for you!

If weights are not for you but you wish to maintain aerobic fitness, take junior out for a walk in the pram or stroller, or walk along a beach with baby in a sling or on shoulders in one of those groovy backpacks. This should swiftly get the heart rate up and if you're looking for extra baby bonus points ask Mum if there's anything required from the shops. While you are secretly adding weight to the load and thereby intensifying your workout, you will appear to be the perfectly 'supportive' parent and there'll be more open acknowledgment of you as a great father.

Remember, at all times though, when exercising with baby, these three important rules:

1 Never exercise on a full stomach. Not yours — the baby's! Up and down movements will invariably release a stomach full of mashed peas, yoghurt, cheese, milk and banana, all of which has been sweetly fermenting and curdling in your baby's tum. A gutful delivered warm and steaming onto your face may send your child into fits of giggles but will probably leave you dry retching and gagging for air.
2 For maximum benefit, all movements should be slow and controlled. Your baby should never be swung, bounced, dropped or thrown through a hoop!
3 It's only common courtesy when you've finished with your baby to wipe it dry of any sweat, should Mum or other members of the family be warming up for a workout after you.

DON'T WORRY ...I'LL TAKE GOOD CARE OF LITTLE HUMPTY!

Chapter 16

Relatives — Who Can You Trust?

There is a theory that the evolution of our species — quite apart from opposable thumbs, big brains and tool making ability — has been assisted by the development of the extended family: brothers, sisters, aunts, uncles and grandparents. The theory goes something like this: with humans living longer, responsibility for the care and upbringing of babies became shared, particularly by aunts and grandmothers past their own childbearing age. This allowed the younger female members of the tribe to get on with hunting, gathering and producing the next generation.

Having your relatives care for your child may not be the smartest option however. We assume that since we survived long enough to reproduce, that the people who brought us into the world must know a thing or two about how to keep a baby happy and healthy. Not necessarily! I believe luck plays a crucial part in anyone's survival.

To prove this for yourself, take the time to sit down with your parents, aunts, uncles, older brothers or sisters, look them straight in the eye and ask the following tricky questions without giving them time to think on their answers. When I was a baby did you ever:

- drop me?
- lose me?
- forget to feed me?
- forget me while shopping and wander away?
- allow me to roll off the bed?
- leave me unattended with a dog?
- leave me unattended in a car?
- dip my dummy in wine or brandy to 'help' me sleep?
- fail to notice me put something in my mouth I might have choked on?
- buy toys for me made of small pieces and clearly marked 'For ages 3 and older'?
- dress me in matching seersucker sailor suit and cap?
- get drunk or just a little 'tipsy' while caring for me?
- smoke cigarettes where I could inhale secondary smoke?

- leave my face covered in apple sauce, milk, custard, yoghurt, peanut butter or chocolate and then take a photo?

If the answer to any of the above is 'Yes' (and I'm sure you can think of plenty of additional questions that relate specifically to your own babyhood), then you seriously need to think about leaving your bub with relatives. Maybe it's these kind of repressed memories that trigger a new parent's complete lack of faith in anybody else to correctly handle their own newborn.

Even if the doting grandparents have had a dozen of their own children and countless other grandchildren up to this point, you will find yourself tense and hovering closely whenever they are holding your baby. You'll feel, in fact, like one of those highly skilled volleyball players waiting to dive forward in an instant — willing to absorb any physical pain your fall to earth may bring, so long as the ball doesn't hit the ground. Though you probably have zero idea of right from wrong in the baby-holding stakes yourself, you will find this urge to be ready for the worst a strong one. Even as your parents stare at you like a dimwitted fool for not trusting their ability to handle a newborn, *you will not trust these people*.

The good thing is that in time you will, out of physical and mental necessity, learn to trust (or if you're an only child, to 'share'). Nature has designed a way that forces you to ease your over-protective grip, to overcome this crisis of faith ... and it's for your own sanity's sake. After thirty-eight consecutive sleepless nights you will gladly hand your child to its grandparents, aunts or uncles, your friendly neighbourhood post person or any door-knocking Mormons who happen to be passing by!

In the early days, however, this tense feeling that no one else can care for your precious baby as carefully as you can dominates your brain. It's similar to the feeling you would have if someone asked to pick up your new $10,000 crystal vase. Let's face it, baby is almost as delicate and you've probably just forked out that much to obstetricians, anaesthetists and GPs for blood tests, referrals to specialists, scanning this, imaging that, clothes, formulas, prams, nappies and all the rest. You certainly wouldn't want someone dropping what is possibly your single biggest ever investment and having it shatter into a thousand pieces on the floor in front of you.

Make no mistake, times and attitudes have changed dramatically since we were babies. What was acceptable in our parents' day is, in many instances, now looked upon as bordering on neglect, if not downright abuse. Take laws requiring baby seats, harnesses and seat belts in cars for instance. We had nothing like that in the 1960s and 1970s when I was a kid. About the best we could hope for was that Mum had a firm enough grip to prevent us flying out the window, as Dad hurtled along the highway in a vehicle designed not for safety or to absorb impact, but rather for invading neighbouring countries.

Forget your airbags and crumple zones, when I was a kid it wasn't that long since 'Double-ya Double-ya Two' and cars were still being designed as potential weapons rather than modes of transport! I particularly remember the proud look upon my father's face the day he crashed into the rear of a stationary bus, only to get out and find not so much as a dint in his heavy steel bumper, or a scratch on the shiny surface of his car. No Nazi commander of a Leopard tank speeding over the tops of peasant villages in small Eastern European countries ever felt as much thrill of accomplishment. For we passengers, the whiplash eventually faded.

Looking back as a kid who survived this reckless era I remember the fun of sliding around the back seat of the car and body slamming my friends against the door when we went round corners, but all that's changed. For babies these days it's reversible polyurethane capsules with velcro webbing and car seats with enough padding and harnessing that they wouldn't look out of place in a space shuttle. And that's as it should be. But for the grandparents this may seem all a little too namby-pamby.

'Whatta ya wanna go spoiling the child for already? You never had any of this malarkey when you where a baby and you turned out all right.' (Which, when you think about it, is a miracle.)

This new world full of regulations and legislation designed to protect the innocent can take a while for the grandparents to adjust to ... they who remember traversing continents in covered wagons! It's interesting to watch the difference in grandmothers and grandfathers too.

Grandmothers will rush straight in for the baby and immediately begin fussing and clucking and singing happy songs, jollying baby along, pushing away anxious and neurotic new mothers and fathers and 'shoo-shooing' newfangled ideas that weren't available when they were parents. Ideas like baby moisturisers ('What's wrong with Vaseline?') and wet wipes ('Here, here, just spit on a hanky and wipe it away!'). For grandmothers the way they did it was good enough for their kids, so it should damn well be good enough for their grandkids as well.

Grandfathers, on the other hand, stand back a bit, usually with a knowing smirk on their faces. 'Ah yes,' they think to themselves, 'Now it's *your* turn to try and tell her how to do it.'

They sit back and wait to be asked before venturing an opinion. Remember they've been there before. They've been put in their place many a time when it comes to right and wrong with baby. They already know they're simple drones and are comfortable in their own skin. You see, they've seen cuts and bruises before, they've seen what too much pureed fruit can do to a nappy, they know how far a vomit can hurl. To them this is the domain of the 'woman', at least it was in their day and to them … it still is!

In fact, grandfathers are almost too comfortable and relaxed with baby. They tend to adopt the 'what doesn't kill 'em makes 'em stronger' position. If a baby, taking its first hesitant and uncertain footsteps outside, falls over on the gravel driveway leaving its face a bloodied pulp, its grandfather will dismiss it as just a scratch. 'It probably won't even leave a permanent mark.' And that's for a girl! If it's a baby boy there'll be the, 'Hey a few scars are good for a man. Means he's not a pansy!' In a grandfather's world, babies never really hurt themselves because, 'They're designed to bounce!'

By and large, grandparents will do either one of two things: rush in to try to take over, or sit back and watch. Either way, with grandparents you can feel confident that their efforts are at least well intentioned. If you have grown up with brothers and sisters, however, things are a little different.

Aunts and particularly uncles believe it is their job to continue the teasing, snitching, fighting and sibling rivalry that characterised their own childhood with you or your partner. These are the people who feel that they must buy your baby the noisiest, most aggravating and irritating toys available: toys with sirens; toys with loud musical chimes; toys that emit ear-splitting sound effects; even toys as simple and unbearably distracting as a whistle. If you think that sounds petty, take it from me ... when baby works out the rudimentary basics of blowing into a whistle, then it knows only one way to do it — it fills those little lungs to capacity and then it blows, flat out. It's a whistle blast that can shatter an eardrum at a distance of twenty feet, let alone the up close and personal treatment baby seems to prefer — like when you're sleeping on the lounge or trapped in a car where the sound has no escape and bounces around for a while.

These toys purchased by aunts and uncles are not for the enjoyment of the child, but for the aggravation they know will be caused to their siblings. It's like a game of 'knuckles' or 'paper, rock, scissors' that has never ended. For people who do this to you it is not a sin to wish twins upon them in the future. Tell them you have a long memory, and that you will be doubly revenged every birthday and Christmas to come.

And while having your own family hanging around so much may become trying, for baby it is akin to being a god. There's so many people to pay attention to you, indulge you and allow you to get away with things your parents are trying to stop you doing. There's hugs and kisses and plenty of people to cater to your every whim — picking up dropped toys, offering you food and drink, wiping up spills and mess. To paraphrase Mel Brooks, 'It's good to be God.' At this age, baby believes it's the smartest thing in the world, that it's able to control everything around it with a smile, or an ear-splitting yell if it doesn't get what it wants.

At the dinner table, when you're a god in your high chair with all the grown-ups around, things really get exciting. Despite baby's inability to speak, all of baby's disciples have learnt to read sign language. Baby–god holds its hands up in the air, and all the grown-up worshippers do the same thing. Put them down again, and all the adults drop their hands at your command. Up, down, up, down, up down for as long as you like, and all the while your faithful followers are laughing along and enjoying the magnificence of being in your company. You are a baby in charge of the universe.

Speaking of your baby's disciples, if you are going to have your child christened or undergo a 'naming day' ceremony, you need to carefully choose your godparents because there's no changing your mind down the track — no trying to exchange them for something more useful like an electric can opener!

These people are welded to your child for life. This wasn't something my wife and I clearly understood until the day of our baby's christening. My best friend was asked to be godfather and the baby's aunt (my wife's sister) was asked to be godmother, to which they both graciously agreed.

The godfather-to-be turned up on the day of this solemn occasion nursing a splitting hangover and stinking like a brewery. I looked into his red-rimmed eyes and smelt the acrid tang of stale alcohol from the night before, even though he'd cunningly tried to disguise the scent by downing a couple of quick drinks just before the ceremony. 'Nerve settlers, mate,' he smiled weakly, then wandered off to make an impression on some of the single female friends of the family who had turned up for the occasion.

'Well really, why would I have expected anything more from him?' I thought to myself. 'At least the

bub's godmother can be relied on for the future!'

It was then quickly on to the ceremony itself which brought enough unexpected distraction to stop my ponderings on the ill choice we had made for our son's godfather, and to begin pondering about God himself.

The priest was welcoming and gentle and the pews were filled with smiling relatives and friends. Our baby, who was at the crawling stage by this time, was happy in Daddy's arms and behaving magnificently ... until it came time to be sprinkled with holy water from a silver goblet, freshly drawn from the baptismal font. Now, if you've ever been in a car accident or similar dangerous situation, you'll be aware of how the world around you seems to slow down. In this instance, baby was so violently opposed to being soaked in this manner that, for the first time ever, the cup the priest was holding, brimming with holy water, was kicked clean out of his hands by a well aimed chubby leg! A hushed murmur went through the crowd, the priest stared wide-eyed then trembled imperceptibly while baby smiled an unnerving smile.

'That's a bad omen,' I thought to myself, although I quickly regained my own sense of humour when the silence in the congregation was broken with laughter and smiles. 'A good little footballer in the making,' was the general consensus.

Then, all of a sudden, it was photo time. The baby, the proud parents, the waste of space godfather and the thankfully more than capable godmother. Perhaps it was the flashing of lightbulbs, perhaps baby had been handed around from one too many adoring relatives and friends throughout the day, or perhaps it was the suffocating stench of his godfather's breath, but right then and there baby discharged the entire contents of his gut. Luckily we'd been expecting something of this nature (although not quite in this quantity) and had placed a cute ducky-wucky bib around our baby's neck.

'Oops! Who's had a little vomee-wommy?' said his new godmother. 'Don't worry you guys I'll fix it up,' she said to us and with a warm, loving smile and with sparkling eyes she reached out to take baby.

'Wow,' I thought, 'She really is terrific. A natural with kids and what a great mother she'll make herself one day. Exactly the right person to be a godparent, unlike someone else I know,' shooting a disapproving glare at my best friend who, in response to his new godchild's predicament, was trying to stifle his own dry retching.

It wasn't until I turned back to see how godmother was doing that the realisation hit that we'd made *two* dreadful choices with our baby's godparents. Godmother, having had no children of her own and therefore being totally oblivious to baby attire (or obviously any comprehension of the most basic laws of physics), had attempted to simply pull the bib up and over our darling's head, rather than untying and removing the bib after securing the steamy, sticky contents wrapped up inside.

Our beautiful baby, on this very special and memorable day, was now covered with puke from the chin on its precious little face to the sweet, wispy hair on the crown of his head.

'What had we been thinking?' I thought as I looked at my baby, its beautiful angelic face and hair covered in a thick smear of its own tacky, up-chucked goop. His godmother was cheekily giggling at what she'd done giving us a ditsy, cutesy-pie, 'Oops. Now that doesn't look right. Sorry!', only stupefying us both further when she said nonchalantly, 'By the way, you both know I'm an atheist, don't you?'

These were the two people we had entrusted with our child's spiritual development and wellbeing, and who would possibly take on the task of baby's complete upbringing should some unforeseen tragedy ever overtake us both.

I went in search of the priest to see if we could retract our choice of godparents or get a refund or something. When I found him however, he was face down in front of the altar, stretched out like a crucifix and mumbling incoherently about the 'number of the beast'. I quickly realised the kicking of the holy water had, as I suspected, not been a favourable portent, and that now wasn't a good time to try and chat.

So remember, you can choose your friends (and even then you can make mistakes) ... but there's nothing baby can do about the extended family inflicted upon it. With all you know about your relatives you need to ask yourself: is this really fair? Doesn't your child deserve better than you had? With this in mind you may decide for baby's overall long-term wellbeing that now *is* the perfect time for that change of lifestyle you've always dreamed about, time to pack up and go experience a simpler way of life ... like living with nomadic tribes on the windswept plains of the Uzbekistani steppe!

THIS LITTLE THING WE ARE MAKING WILL BRING US CLOSER TOGETHER... JUST MAYBE NOT IN THE PHYSICAL SENSE!

Chapter 17

Sex – Those Were the Days

Like a fair percentage of sex itself, I'll keep this brief!

'Sex' is a pleasant interlude where pre-parents have fun playing with each other's genitals in order to pass spare time. Unfortunately, as a parent you no longer have 'pleasant interludes' because:

1 You have no spare time;
2 If you do have spare time The Boss will always find you something more important to do (like disinfecting bath toys!);
3 You are so traumatised by the harrowing series of events that have led you to becoming a parent (look at what happened last time you had sex!) that Mr-Happy-In-Your-Pants isn't so sure he wants to come out and play any more; or
4 If you have time for sex, then you have time for sleep, and as a parent, sleep always wins!

Can't believe a man would choose sleep over sex? Read on ...

WOW...THEY GET OLD SO QUICKLY!

Chapter 18

Sleeping

Night time. This is the time most people in the world sleep. For new parents this is no longer the case. New parents do not sleep. They try to sleep, they desperately want to sleep but ... baby has other ideas.

To understand why, you need to see things from the baby's perspective. It's just survived nine months in a cramped, dark place, so when the lights are turned off and it goes quiet, what's to stop baby thinking it's about to get shoved back into what it had such a hell of a time getting out of?

'No way people — put the lights back on, get in here and let me know I'm not about to be sucked back up that thing. And bring me some food while you're at it ... and that rattle whatsit I like shaking around ... and a dry nappy OK, 'cause I'm up to my armpits in this one!'

Plus, it's boring lying on your back looking up at the same old dangly things that aren't doing anything 'cause there's no one around to push or bounce them. There's no music, no TV, you can't order out for a pizza. It's dull, dull, dull. What is required is one of those parent people that sing silly songs, make funny faces and dance around kind of weird and stupid-like.

Yes, for babies and toddlers, 'night time' is just the same as 'play time'. And if night time play time doesn't get your attention then night time 'vomit time' surely will. This, for parents, becomes 'Oh my God, what's wrong with the baby?' time, followed by an hour of 'changing the pyjamas, changing the sheets, changing the blankets, changing the pillow case, changing the pillow and settling the baby back down ... just in time for it to puke up again all over the clean new sheets, blankets, pillow, pyjamas and you' time.

And when it comes to being sick, babies have a built-in preference for night time visitations. Just as turtles instinctively crawl towards the sea after they've hatched, babies have a preference for being sick after hours, particularly on a Sunday night when the doctor's rates are way up.

Anyway, there are plenty of other books and

people to tell you how little sleep parents get. What you need to know are the 'up' sides of sleep deprivation ... To tell the truth there are none because you're usually so exhausted you wouldn't be able to enjoy any of them anyway, but here's something that might help.

Before fatherhood, real men never leave work early. You know it's crucial for you to be seen to work twenty-five hours a day, eight days a week.

'Yeah, I stayed at work till midnight finishing the annual report, watched the late, late news, current affairs and finance update, read a Tom Clancy novel till 4, grabbed a bit of sleep, got up and went for a jog and a swim, squeezed in some boxercise and was in the office by 5 to clinch that London deal.'

Sleep is for wimps!

Being a new dad, however, provides one of the very few excuses workmates will allow you to jump off this crushing testosterone treadmill. Workmates allow this 'out' because we all secretly lie to each other about how much time we put in anyway. Plus, we know from what we've heard and read that being a parent *really can* lead to sleep deprivation psychosis. None of us wants to become the next victim of a bloke with a shotgun and a grudge against his workplace because they didn't let him off early every once in a while!

So with the excuse of having to 'help with the

baby' you can actually go home at least 'on time' to the place and the people you really want to be with, and if everything works out you can be in bed with a cup of warm milk before the cheesy news anchor's patronising, 'That's the news *that* is the news. I'm Alan Autocue. Goodnight.'

To accommodate parents' needs, many restaurants have something most men have never heard of. They call it 'early seating'. That is, they open at around 6 p.m. (just when any real man is rolling the sleeves up for another few hours of boardroom negotiations and meetings with international investment bankers). While most pre-parents are either still at work or downing a few after work, somnambulant fathers head out into the early evening with their babies and 'living dead' partners in what is often a vain attempt to enjoy a meal and each other's company.

They head out early for two reasons:

1 The possibility they may still be awake by the time dessert is served; and
2 So as not to disturb *others*.

'Others'. That's what we parents call people without children! 'Others' ... it's like some malevolent alien race from a 1950s B-grade movie. There should be dramatic, over-the-top movie music every time you have one of these discussions ...

'Feel like trying to catch a movie? I think baby will sleep through.'

'Yeah but what if he wakes up? He'll disturb all the Others!'

Insert melodramatic B-grade movie music. Daaaaaa da da da dum DUM!

'It'd be great to go to that dinner party at Rob's place but if we take the baby, what about the Others?'

Daaaaaa da da da dum DUM!

'I'd like to fly over and let baby meet the grandparents but if we're on a plane and he starts crying, what about the Others?'

Dum dum dum DUUUUUM!

There's also something else that balances the body-crushing sleep deprivation ledger: baby gives you a permanent, non-threatening, non-offensive excuse for NOT going out.

'Gee Glenda. I was so looking forward to joining you tonight at the avant garde feminist poetry symposium in support of the Azerbaijani Women's Collective ... but the baby is teething.'

Of course 'sleep' is a relative word. When a parent says sleep, it means something very different to what it means to others. For others sleep means closing your eyes and not opening them again for six, seven or eight hours. For parents, sleep can come to mean a 'refreshing and revitalising' eleven minutes passed out half on the lounge and half on the floor, nursery rhyme book between the knees, a partly consumed bottle of milk and a teddy bear in one arm and a baby that's just finally dozed off in the other. Even with you unable to move a muscle for fear of waking the bub, as the cramp intensifies like burning coals in your arms, your back, your neck and the left cheek of your butt, this is a blissful time of rest.

You'll also find the human body is remarkably adaptive. It can compensate for losses. It is well documented that people who lose their sight usually acquire a heightened sense of hearing and smell. In the case of parents a lack of sleep can lead to the development of night vision.

I can now find a dummy in the dark. To a pre-parent this may not sound like such a fabulous skill, yet you will find that night vision is a crucial survival technique in the home — as much as it is an indispensable part of the kit for stealthy military patrols around the world. Picture this: your partner is seriously on the edge of sleep-deprived meltdown. She *will* cause you serious physical damage if you do not ensure the slumbering baby in your arms is placed ever so gently into its cot without waking, so that Mum can get a few hours sleep before the next feed.

Inside your own skull is severe disorientation. Just walking to the baby's room is like staggering along the deck of a ship heaving in a tsunami. The room is quiet and almost totally dark with just a tiny baby light in the corner of the room to show where the walls are. You place the baby softly into the cot, being careful not to bump the edges or drop the bub onto the pillow from too great a height, and then it happens ... On contact with the pillow, the dummy that was in the tot's mouth falls out, drops between the slats and bounces under the cot.

Forget being ambushed by Charlie and having to retreat back to your own fortified position under intense semi-automatic gunfire, mortar barrage and napalm. This is serious! The baby is 'unsettled' and unless that dummy is placed back between lips that are forming for a scream that would wake the dead (not to mention your long-suffering neighbours and borderline psychotic wife), you can expect at least another two hours of merciless and unrelenting story telling and peek-a-boo.

You dive for cover, face down on the floor under the cot, working against time — you have only three seconds before all hell breaks lose!

All about you are long, low, imperceptible shadows cast by the light from that useless two-watt globe on the table three metres away! You can spy the intermingled shadows of a stuffed teddy, a clown doll, a shoe, a piece of week-old dried and shrivelled banana, a dead bug ... and a dummy.

Two seconds to go. Your desperately aching brain starts an internal conflict with itself, 'This is nice, stretched out on the floor here, where it's dark and quiet. What if I lay my head on my arm and close my eyes for just a moment. Maybe baby won't wake up.'

'Are you mad? Get a grip man! You know that won't happen, it never happens. The child *always* wakes. You've seen the signs, you've heard the warning, now grab that dummy!'

Which shadow? Your arm instinctively snaps out in front and your hand grips on ... One second to go. A pre-murmur from the baby. It's almost too late! If you don't get the dummy back in the mouth right now, it's all over. You roll across the floor — just as you learnt in basic training — and with your arms tucked under your chest you push yourself upright and then have the presence of mind to *slowly* reach out and slip the dummy gently between the lips of the baby who, with nanoseconds left before waking, slips back into unconsciousness.

Then the weirdest thing happens. No matter how

diabolically knackered you are, despite the fact that every fibre of every nerve is a taut high-tension wire about to snap, you find yourself staring down at baby, unable to leave until you've had just one last long look, one soft stroke of the hair, one gentle squeeze of the hand ... before realising something is not quite right.

You quietly bend down again, reach out under the cot then stand up, remove the dead bug from your baby's lips and this time put in the dummy.

'It's OK,' you say to yourself, 'No harm done. No one need ever know.'

Mission accomplished, you head back to your own bedroom to lay down and sleep but ... despite feeling as though twenty heavy blankets have been placed on top of you, because you are a man there is a sense of exhilaration and accomplishment in having put baby to sleep. You are slightly 'stirred' by your achievement in the face of imminent danger and so you stretch out a gentle, loving and exploratory hand and touch mummy to see if she is conscious and willing, or at least so deeply asleep she might not notice and ...

'Wah, wah, wah' — *baby interruptus.*

Get used to it!

LOOK HONEY... AN EVENLY BALANCED MEAL! SOME ON THIS SIDE... SOME ON THAT SIDE!

Chapter 19

Feeding

Once baby begins to eat solids, then feeding can become a monstrously erratic and unnerving daily event for most men.

You know your child is hungry. Even if your child isn't hungry you know when it should be. You also know that to be healthy it needs to eat a regular balanced diet to receive all the nutritional value its quickly growing body requires. That's rational. That's logical. But as I've mentioned, logical, rational, man-thought is not always recommended when dealing with babies because of the difficulty this presents for the male brain. Baby sees it differently.

Baby may not be hungry when you rationally decide it should be. Even if it is hungry, it may not want what you're offering. It may not want to be in the highchair. It may not want to wear a bib. It may not want to eat off the spoon. It may not want you to feed it. It may not want to wear the effeminate sailor suit its adoring grandmother bought it. It may not want to be in that room. And it may not want peach-flavoured slop — slop that has been its favourite meal for three weeks now; instead it may want banana-flavoured slop.

Unable to clearly communicate this to you — or, as the baby sees it, your inability to figure out what is obvious — leads to severe, vein blistering tension within the male brain as we grapple with the fact that 'logically' baby should be eating.

'Eat it!' scream your throbbing neurons.

This searing internal conflict is similar to that which occurs when trying to understand why 'real' women watch impossibly thin fashion models, without the slightest feminine curve to their bodies, wander aimlessly along a catwalk wearing clothes designed by gay men.

'Of course the clothes don't look the same on you darling. You have a *woman's* body. You're not built like the 15-year-old boy the designer had in mind!'

The logic seems so obviously apparent and yet they will not see it.

Eventually, baby starts to show some interest in whatever slop is up for grabs and the pulsing throb in your temple starts to subside. Indeed, watching a baby happily eating is another one of the great things about being a parent. There's something fascinating about the whole uncoordinated effort of it all. (Let's face it, feeding time at the zoo is the best part of a visit.)

Speaking of which, we watch a lot of cooking programs in our house. Of course by that I mean The Boss watches a lot of cooking programs, therefore so do I. Dare I say it, while she avidly leans forward in her chair. I tend to glaze over ('glaze', get it? Trying too hard? Yeah, thought so ...).

On one program recently the obligatory overly enthusiastic gastronome was pontificating about food, exuding the usual amount of syrupy tripe (get it? 'Syrupy tripe'? OK, I'll leave off now ...), going on and on about aroma, presentation and the sheer delight he felt when tasting flavour 'fusions', or feeling fishy flesh with his fingers (that's not easy to say!).

I mean, seriously, I watched this guy pour crushed ice on a plate, drop a few bits of rancid seaweed on top and then throw some oysters around it. That was it! Oysters on seaweed-draped ice.

He sniffed at it, looked at it lovingly and said obsequiously, 'Have a look at that! Brilliant isn't it? And hmmmm, smell that scent. That's heavenly's what that is. Looks good, smells great and it's so easy.' Of course it was easy! For God sake he'd dropped some rotting kelp on ice and was going into raptures about the stench. What a tosser!

If you want to see a real food connoisseur, watch your baby. They are the true critics. If it's bad, baby will let you know in no uncertain terms. Food may end up smeared across its face from chin to cranium, but there's no way it's going in baby's mouth if baby doesn't like it. And too bad if it bruises your ego or seems insensitive to the love with which you've prepared the meal. Bad is bad and baby is going to let you know. No need for etiquette or niceties. And if you try again baby will bring up an arm with the timing and speed of an elite athlete, whacking the spoon at just the right angle to send sticky custard hurtling across the floor, the cupboards, the lounge, the dog and your best new business suit — just as you're about to walk out the door for the meeting you're already running late for.

But if they like it ... Watch baby with something as mundane as a piece of toast! Baby doesn't have to worry about manners. A baby can eat free from form and formality. Unfettered from the conventions of knife and fork, conversation and politeness. This is unashamed sensuality. Watch baby marvel over a mashed and masticated morsel.

Food is placed in the mouth, salivated on and softened. Then pulled out all slimy and limp, turned around, inspected from side to side, drooled over and re-inserted. And not just nicely placed back in with forefinger and thumb, pinky raised in the air. No, it gets shoved back in with gusto by an entire open palm, an upward push that sees the gooey mess munched upon by a gummy mouth and a face full of delight.

And why bother to use a spoon when eating yoghurt? It feels so much better to put your whole hand into the tub, thumb and all, right up to the elbow! Tastes just as good licking it off your fingers and when you get excited and shake your hands about, it goes so much further, right across the room and onto the bookshelf!

This, of course, does bring us to the topic of food that is dropped or thrown. There's really nothing much to say other than: expect it, get used to it and don't fight it, otherwise a hemisphere of your brain will haemorrhage.

For bub, hurling food — planned or otherwise — is a terrific pastime, often more enjoyable than the eating itself. There's endless fun and discovery in watching a can of cold spaghetti silently sliding down a cupboard door; enjoyment only matched by the thrill of pouring a bowl of mushy cereal over the side of the high chair and watching the spatters splash in all directions; or there's the enthralling amoebic spectacle of a slowly spreading pool of baked beans, being added to spoonful after spoonful.

You see, you can't house train a baby the way you can a puppy or a kitten or one of those Vietnamese pot-bellied pigs. (And for the record, unless you are a pot-bellied Vietnamese farmer, keeping a pig in the house is not 'sweet', 'different', 'interesting' or 'zany'. It's just plain stupid.) Rolled-up newspapers and noses rubbed in spilled food will quickly have the local social services rapping at the door and anyway, according to the experts, baby is simply 'experimenting' and 'testing the limits'. Forget the experts! As a house-proud father you know your baby is doing it purposely and wilfully because it wants to see your skull cave in again — like it did that time you hadn't slept for seventeen consecutive nights.

All this talk of eating leads us to the topic of teeth — which brings us to teething. The experts seem to be divided into two camps on this. On one side are those who claim that teething is so matter-of-fact and run-of-the-mill for baby that the appearance of teeth is not even noticed by bub. These people would have us believe that baby feels no discomfort or ill effects whatsoever. To their way of thinking the onset of teeth is of so little consequence to the baby that the tooth fairy doesn't take teeth away but rather deposits them in baby's mouth as it slumbers.

On the other side of the argument are the people who claim teething leads to earache, irritability, drooling, nausea, fever, lack of appetite, diarrhoea, vomiting, Third World debt and reality television. In fact, anything that goes wrong with baby, from the time the first pearly white begins poking through to the installation of dentures is due to teething.

Whatever the truth, I tend to fall on the side of the guys who believe that this has got to be, at the very least, an uncomfortable period of time for the baby. Think about it. Baby has nothing but soft, pink gummy tissue covering its jaws where the teeth will eventually be. Suddenly something begins pushing, poking and forcing its way through the underside of this living flesh — and not all teeth are sharp and pointy — those at the front and the sides are big, flat and blunt. To my way of thinking that's gotta be like bamboo-under-the-fingernails torture, as a bloody great tusk tears its way through to the surface. Why wouldn't you get a bit irritable?

When teething, baby starts looking around for things to gnaw on and anything that could soothe the pain gets a thorough sucking. Amongst other things, Mum or Dad's finger is just the ticket. It's not too big, it has a bit of cushioning when you first bite down and then there's a nice hard centre. Finger-gnawing becomes a regular event for most parents who try to soothe their baby's inflamed gums with a gel designed to numb the gum, while allowing bub to also have a bit of a gummy-suckle.

This is all well and good until the teeth actually arrive! Now placing a finger in baby's newly crenellated jaws can lead to severe laceration and mauling. Again, if you're to assist baby through this period, a subtle shift in perception is required. You still need to place a gel-covered finger in baby's mouth, but it's now part of a vicious game of cat and mouse that could leave you minus a limb!

How do you deal with it? Ever fed flies to a Venus flytrap? Just the same! Open baby's mouth, quickly whip your goop-covered finger in and then withdraw before the mandibles close to crush and mutilate your digit.

By the way, your baby can come to love the gel and can quite easily become addicted to it. Sure it helps ease the pain, but that's not the real reason your baby will cry out for more of the stuff (even when its teeth aren't bothering it). You see, it's the same reason that makes grown men drunkenly dice with death, or at least the possibility of singed eyebrows, blistered lips and a swollen tongue. This soothing, numbing gum gel tastes like aniseed.

That's right, just like ouzo! Come to think of it, ouzo has the same kind of numbing effect only *all over*, though that's no excuse to start sucking a tube of gum gel next time the bar is empty!

While we're on teeth and teething, you'll have to become accustomed to another of baby's bodily functions, the production of saliva or 'drool'. Mucus, poo, vomit *and* drool. No, really, who wouldn't want to have a baby?

When the teeth begin turning up, baby will drool even more. Babies drool because they haven't learned to swallow their own saliva. The only way to stop them from drowning in a constant build-up of their own fluid is to let it all just dribble out of their mouths. Clearly this is another baby design fault.

As I've mentioned several times now, dealing with all this baby stuff can be as simple as shifting your perspective, so here's a free tip for someone looking to make a quick fortune. It doesn't matter how antiseptic and spotlessly clean your house is, if there's pet hair or a dust clump anywhere in the vicinity of something your child has slobbered on, you can be sure the hair, dust and dirt will be attracted to it. Forget your swisher mops and electro-static-picker-upperer broom things. Cover something in baby goop, dribble or drool, mop your floors and they'll look like new. I swear that if you bottled this stuff in industrial quantities someone could make a fortune!

And since we're talking about entrepreneurs and bodily fluids, remember in the previous chapter we talked about mucus? Well, here's another tip for some ingenious marketing person to grab hold of (but remember to credit me with the idea and 30 per cent of the profit).

Babies produce literally buckets of mucus, right? So what to do with it rather than just wiping the goop up and tipping it out? Well, you might feel I'm being overly gross here but to my mind this is just another time to flick the perspective switch. How about we produce another product:

Mucus moisturiser! *Oil of Goll-ay*.

Think about it: women will smear any repugnant, repellent and revolting lotion on their body, face and arms without a second thought, as long as it has a French sounding name, a perfumed scent and it claims to make them look younger. They never read the ingredients on the label, and some of these companies are so smart they don't print any ingredients so as to safeguard their 'secret formula'. More likely it's to stop people gagging at the thought of what they're emolliating themselves with, because it's well known fact that perfumes and chick lotions are made from some weird stuff.

Without a word of a lie, here's some of the stuff that goes into perfumes. Are you ready? Castoreum resin from beavers! Musk from musk deer! A gland secretion from the civet cat and ... wait for it ... stuff called 'ambergris'. Know what that is? It's the phlegm coughed up by sperm whales! I kid you not, look it up in the dictionary.

Let's face it, if they're prepared to spritz or smear themselves with any of this (or even something as mundane as mud), *why not mucus*?

Disgusting concept, I grant you, but since love of your newborn will overcome your fear of bodily excretions, you may as well use this newfound strength for good. So since you'll have a ready supply at hand, what's to stop you placing a label on an attractively designed little bottle, adding a dash of perfume and colouring, giving it a sophisticated French-sounding name (such as Muco de Bebe), and making some outlandish and unsupportable claim about the 100 per cent 'natural' ingredients? 'Voilà!' Fame, fashion and fortune await.

DROP.... DROP ...DROP!
KICK... KICK ...KICK
KICK KICK K..I..C..K
DROP KICK!
GOLDIN

Chapter 20

Talking

By the time your child is able to hold a conversation you will notice your own speaking skills have dramatically improved. In particular, your 'articulation'. Your pronunciation and diction will be far more crisp and rounded in delivery. You may even roll your Rs and your language will take on the tone of a Shakespearean 'ac-tor'.

Why? Because of repetition. With a new baby you go out of your way to teach it how to say things and you therefore repeat words over and over ... and over .... and over. You will also go out of your way to say those words clearly, precisely and confidently. Indeed, you are like an 'ac-tor' delivering the words with an overly dramatic aplomb. And like an 'ac-tor' you start to say even the most mundane words in every different style and tempo the human tongue can form.

Upward inflections, flat and sing-song; sometimes sharp and fast, at other times long and drawn out; and all the time repeated over and over again in a never-ending sentence, as you attempt to have the word and its meaning burn into the memory of your child.

'That's the car; Daddy's car. Caaar. Car! Can you say "car"? Caaaaaaaaar. Car! Car! The car. Daddy's car. You say it! You say "caaaaaar".'

In all probability the child will stare at you blankly or perhaps turn and watch something more interesting than its droning father. However, if it makes any kind of audible noise (even if it's only a belch or a digestive tract clearance), then whether it was trying to talk or not, you will latch onto that sound as a sure sign your child is extraordinarily gifted and obviously way ahead of any other kid its age! And because you've read all the 'correct' books about bringing up a child, where the experts tell you to always react in a positively reinforcing manner with your baby, you say:

'Good, good. Yes! That's right! Car! The car. Daddy's car. Good. Can you say it again? Car! Can you say "car"? Car. You try it again. Caaaar. Don't want to? OK we'll drop it for now. Give it a rest. You did very well though.'

And then, because you just can't resist the hope

that maybe your genius baby will say it again, you throw one more in for good measure.

'Car.'

And it's not just words that get repeated over ... and over .... and over .... and over. It's songs ... and books.

You may have noticed there are not too many geniuses that have their 'eureka' breakthrough moments after the age of thirty. Why should that be? It's because by then most people have had, or are in relationships, and *relationships* are draining.

Dinners, movies, walks on the beach and babies take an enormous amount of time and energy away from the fascinating research of quantum physics, the reproductive organs of starfish or any other research that necessitates the kind of deep and relentless focus required to make you forget you're not getting laid ... ever! (It's a fact that Sir Isaac Newton was celibate.)

If the relationship has produced a 'viable biological outcome' — a baby — then time for self-indulgent exploration of desert sands for the ancestral forebears of homo erectus gargantua pretty much dries up in an endless tedium of feeding, burping and changing.

You know, you're only born with so many brain

cells and those that may have been equipped to deal with philosophical metaphor or clever conversation with friends about existentialism (or any kind of thing with an 'ism' at the end of it), are the same ones that have to deal with *Bongo Goes for a Walk*.

If you're used to getting out of tricky situations you don't understand by looking disdainfully and saying, 'It's all so banal isn't it?', or if you're used to sprouting phrases like, 'According to Kafka', or 'I feel Dostoevski's third movement of the first concerto is a metaphor for conveying the primordial feeling of retrograde latent Marxism in a triumphant swirl of totalitarian schizophrenic proletarian dogma' — then make the most of what brain cells you have left, because they're about to turn to mush.

Look, I know that in this computer-literate age we need to teach kids to read and be comfortable with books, but after baby has demanded you read the same book for the 15,000th time — even though there's a whole heap of others to choose from — the constant dripping of the Chinese water torture makes you understand why some people *choose* insanity.

'Swish, swish, swish. It's fun to be a fish.'

Well, let me tell you, it may be fun to be a fish but as a parent you just wish someone, somewhere had pulled the author of these books out of whatever scum-filled pond they live in, cut their heads off and gutted them. I know it's a bit Jeffrey Darmer-ish, but you will come to understand what I'm about when you wake at ten past three in the morning for no other reason than your brain cannot clear itself of, 'I'm gonna shake, shake, shake my sillies out ... wiggle my waggles away.'

And babies can be cruel. Just when you start to relax because finally junior is indicating interest in one of its other books, you realise it's just another title from the same series!

Bongo Learns to Count.

Bongo Finds a Friend.

Bongo Digs a Hole.

What about *Bongo Visits the Vet ... and Doesn't Come Back!*?

You see, for baby, repetition isn't monotonous — in fact, it's new and interesting every time. The theory is that the memory part of the brain is like a muscle. And like muscle it needs to be used and worked before it begins to function properly. With so much to take in every time you're conscious, the brain takes a while to actually start figuring out how to operate the memory function — what is important to make note of for future reference and what is not.

In fact, a new bub's memory is little more

advanced than a goldfish. There is a school of thought (Get it? School of thought? OK, OK ... no more of that) which believes goldfish happily live in bowls because their memories only last as long as it takes to do a lap. Each time they swim a circuit, the scene to them is new and interesting. (Or was that an episode of Seinfeld? Hell, what a world we live in when credible scientific research and a sit-com become confused.)

Frustrating as it may be when baby doesn't seem to remember things you did half an hour ago (or when you notice you can't pronounce 'antidisestablishmentarianism' any more), there is a certain satisfaction before their memory begins to function. For instance, you'll be able to keep your baby spellbound for hours playing 'Where is it?' Pull something out from under a blanket (where you placed it only twenty seconds before) and see the look of amazement and joy on its face. Turn baby around to look at something else, bring its attention back, pull out the toy from under the blanket and guess what? Baby gets excited and amazed all over again!

If you're having a bad day and need to feel a little special, babies are the deal. That's right! Daddy is soooo clever and soooo funny and soooo smart ... and handsome! (Well maybe not the handsome bit but you get where I'm coming from!)

With all this language theory you become aware that babies are a lot smarter than people used to give them credit for. It's now believed they can even pick up on nuance and tone while still inside the uterus. (No we didn't start reading the alphabet or playing Tchaikovsky to our unborn baby, although I do recall cupping my hands around my mouth like a megaphone and yelling into my wife's swelling tummy once or twice, 'Hey in there! This is the Rolling Stones.')

Early on, however, we were careful not to say *bad* words around the baby and that extended to having no arguments or fights around our bub. This is *obviously* a totally unnatural state for any normal male and female, and brings with it added frustration, tension and irritability. That's right, pretending to be perfect is just what you need on top of the insecurity of being a new parent, sleep deprivation and concerns about money. Cynicism and sarcasm quickly becomes the norm.

When having a 'spat', you will find you and your partner begin talking *through* your child. You will talk in ways designed to cause hurt to each other but all delivered with sugary sweetness so as not to let the 'tone' of the conversation distress the little person.

'Mummy has to remind Daddy again that he

hasn't taken the rubbish out. He's a silly Daddy isn't he diddums?'

'Mummy forgot she asked Daddy to go to the shops and, if she'd bothered to notice, she would have seen Daddy was just about to take the rubbish out now, wasn't he snookums?'

'That's strange! Daddy, sitting on his fat behind staring at sport on telly, doesn't look like the rubbish being taken out, does it bubby? Not to mention, since coming back from the shops, he's left the door open again so those nasty little flysey wiseys can settle on your food and give you dysentery wysentery. Daddy's a thoughtless, insensitive piggy, isn't he sweety? Can you make a pig noise? Do you remember what noise a pig makes? That's right, "Oink! Oink!" Daddy's an oink oink piggy wiggy isn't he?'

Then there's the speech variation you will need to come to terms quickly — one my friend Dave calls the 'observational command'. This is when your wife or partner makes a statement of fact that is actually a command, a command you are meant to respond to with swift, affirmative action. Since the little lady will resort to this speech pattern as soon as she is tired, worn out or just annoyed with you (for no particular reason other than you seem to be relaxed without permission), you need to quickly train yourself to pick up on its particular nuance if you wish to avoid her inflicting you with a crippling physical disability.

'The baby has a dirty nappy!'

Replying with, 'Yeah I thought I smelled something,' while continuing to watch the Miss Universe pageant on TV is not what she wants to hear.

'The baby needs to be fed!'

Looking up from the newspaper and saying, 'Oh, good 'cause I'm starving. And what's for dinner anyway?' is again, not what she wants to hear.

You see, she is not making vague conversation and generally enjoying your company. Rather, she is *telling* you to do something and to do it *now* ... or feel the sting of her six-inch stilettos in the back of your head.

Then after a while, just sometimes, the sarcasm, threats and vicious barbs from your wife or partner start to mingle in your mind with all the poo, vomit, mucus and thrown food. You look at the tiny terrorist who has taken total control of *your* home — a home under siege — and ask yourself, 'Whose house is this anyway?' You even remember it wasn't all that long ago you really weren't all that thrilled about babies. But then — in a flash — nature has a way of balancing things out.

You see it doesn't matter whether baby is trying

to say 'dog' or 'dumb' or 'dolt' or 'D'oh!' All you'll hear is 'Da-da', because nature has made 'D' one of the easier letters to say. Much, much easier than say the letter 'M'.

Your silent revenge for sucking up hours of sarcastic abuse with a smile is the knowledge that every time baby says 'Da-da' (or anything that can be interpreted as 'Da-da'), insane jealousy is just burning up inside of Mum, desperately waiting for baby to say 'Ma-ma'. Thank you *Father* nature.

Chapter 21

Getting Around

For the first six months you will cajole and encourage your baby to take control of the machine within which it exists. You will urge it to crawl, talk, reach out and grab things. In encouraging baby, you will behave in ways that make you look like you are, in fact, certifiable.

You will speak in stupid voices, you will make weird faces, blow air bubbles like a gold fish, do the rubber-band dance, spin your eyes, wave your arms and sing novelty songs from the 1950s. You will recall things you haven't done since you were in primary school, like turning your eyelids inside out.

Obviously, from baby's perspective, watching your parent bounce about on the spot, marching, crawling, picking things up, singing songs and reciting poems is nothing short of a cruel tease, highlighting its own inadequacy.

4X4
A
C
GOLDING

'Sure, I'm struggling with the basic motor skill of placing one foot in front of the other, but gee thanks for pointing out my deficiencies. No, I'll be all right. I won't need therapy. I won't want to sue you in later life for psychological and emotional abuse ... or maybe I will!'

You, on the other hand, will be constantly taking photos and rejoicing every time baby does something more coordinated than it did the day before. You will spend hours explaining to grandparents, aunts, uncles, friends and old ladies at bus shelters how your baby did anything that could be considered 'controlled'.

Funny thing is, as soon as baby starts achieving success in any of the things you have been desperately trying to assist it with, you will say:

'No!'

'Don't.'

'Sit still.'

'Be quiet.'

'Don't touch.'

'Don't put that in your mouth.'

'Leave it alone!!!'

And this must set up bone-jarring confusion in baby's young mind. But the interesting thing is that babies are all so matter-of-fact about what they achieve.

One day you will find that baby has gone from useless, wriggling thing, kicking arms and legs about in the air while you barrack from the sidelines urging it on, to confidently crawling about on hands and knees and able to pull itself up as if it's been capable of this all along — and there's nothing special about it anyway.

Then before you know it, baby has the motor skills to lift itself up and inspect the inside of its toy box, while you watch from a distance. If it doesn't empty the entire contents of the box onto itself in the process, the next thing that will happen is baby will try climbing in, fixated on a specific object. As it pulls itself up, all kind of clumsy and ungainly, it will reach the point beyond perpendicular — and topple in head first. (To be truthful I have no reference point for this in baby girls. For all I know only boys do this because, let's face it, boys grow into men who continue doing physically stupid things well past when a smart brain would say 'stop now'.)

What's amazing is that the now-upside-down baby in the box will wriggle and squirm and flay its arms and legs and eventually sit upright, surrounded by all its toys, a nonplussed expression on its face, unfazed and detached from what it has achieved. It is completely unaware of the Everest it has conquered in righting itself, as it goes on hunting for the toy it has decided must be found.

You, on the other hand, will assume the expression of a rabbit in headlights, totally stunned at your baby's achievement. You, who has been encouraging and assisting for months on end, will race for the nearest camera or video, will be calling relatives (again) and inviting the CNN news crew to come and mark this historic event for posterity.

So, baby is now sitting in the toy box totally absorbed in its search, looking like it's capable of doing anything it wants to do, picking up toys, inspecting and rejecting them. What is it looking for?

The expensive spinning gizmo? No, that gets dropped over the edge.

What about the wobbling, musical, shaking thingy? No ... gone.

Could it be the flashing-light whatsit? That gets discarded over the side so quickly baby doesn't even watch it fall.

Maybe the exciting, spinning, singing, multicoloured, pull-apart stacker doover? No, not even a second glance.

Of all the fabulous, colourful, musical, squishy, warm and cuddly things, what does baby find most fascinating? One of Dad's old runners, inadvertently scooped up during the previous evening's sleep deprived haze of tidying. And why wouldn't baby like playing with one of these things? Have a look at them from a baby's perspective. Laces are long and dangly. It's made of different bits of material that feel good on the gums and taste interesting to the tongue. Rubber soles with funny contours to play with and prise muck out of with little fingers, and the whole shoe is lightweight yet sturdy. It doesn't fall apart and doesn't hurt if you whack yourself in the face with it. They smell kind of funny too and you can poke half your head right inside one! Now that's gotta be more fun than the antiseptically clean, smooth, new plastic toy that doesn't do anything but make the same boring rattle noise when you push it!

Before you know it baby is walking around and putting hands on 'this', placing 'that' in its mouth, reaching up and poking fingers into everything. Soon enough, baby is capable of getting around the whole house and that includes the bathroom, which brings us to the dilemma of the toilet seat — up or down?

The age-old quest of women around the planet has been to get men to lower the toilet seat after a python siphon. From the male perspective the toilet looks just the same lid up or down, plus, by leaving it up it's prepared for the next time we need to shake hands with the wife's best friend. No bending the back all the time lifting up what needn't have been put down in the first place! The problem is that women have been unable to find a logical, rational reason for why we should put it down. Instead, they always resort to the ease and comfort of abuse and denigration.

'Oh that's disgusting', and 'You're revolting', and 'It just makes me sick'. All of which to us men, of course, is like a badge of honour, something to make us stick our chests out and strut about.

Well you know what? I now put the toilet seat down. *Voluntarily*. Why? Because little hands have a great love of slipping along smooth porcelain surfaces and delving about in there. Not to mention inquisitive, oversized heads that can topple the rest of the body in. So there you go. It hasn't been that hard for me to make the transition. Like all men I just needed a *rational* reason for doing it.

Once baby has progressed from crawling to toddling you will be able to observe evolution in action. Little hands freed up can now manipulate tools, one of the greatest achievements of MAN-kind. Using tools allowed us to adapt our environment for our own needs, utilising materials around us to gain an ascendancy over the brute animals. It is one of the things that allow us to dominate.

So what do you think was the first tool? Documentaries of primitive man and modern day chimpanzees give us tantalising hints. Was it the flint to make fire? The stone axe head for hunting and carving? Sharp-edged, palm-sized tools for cutting, scraping and breaking bones. I believe it was none of these.

My theory of the very first tool and its use is based on careful observation of the wild eleven-month-old toddler in its home environment. I figured it out while watching from a safe vantage point as the 'animal' walked around hitting anything that looked interesting with a wooden spoon in one hand and a plastic spatula in the other. He bashed the lounge, the stereo, the bookshelf, the slumbering dog and yes, no matter how many times he'd been told not to, he stretched up and tried to insert the spatula into the rotating blades of the nearby pedestal fan spinning at 3000 revs per minute. Everything he whacked was new, interesting and good for a laugh.

So what then was the first tool? I don't think it was anything to do with survival — I think it was made for fun. No matter how many times Cro-Magnon kid's parents told him not to, the first tool was probably a sharp stick, just the right size for a toddler hand to take firm grip of and shove up the backside of the nearest baboon.

Chapter 22

Blokes, Babies and Babes

Once a son is born, new mothers come to a deeper and more fundamental understanding of the male psyche. They find within themselves a far greater connection with their men. They come to more fully appreciate just what it is to be a male; of what it is to be full of testosterone! This awakening happened with my wife after the first couple of months.

One day she came over to me and softly sat down. While holding my hand in a firm but gentle grip, she looked deep into my eyes for a long moment. She kept staring and nodded slowly with a subtle hint of a smile.

I thought I must have been in really big trouble! Immediately guilt filled me for whatever it was I

THE SUBTLE CHANGE OF A BLOKE WITH A BABY
UG
HUG
GOLDING

hadn't done. What was she getting at? What did she want? She continued with something I had rarely seen. My wife was being truly sincere. From a place deep, deep within herself she quietly said, 'I understand. Finally I really do understand. Not only do I understand, but importantly I accept.'

Now I was really getting edgy. This supportive, nurturing talk out of the blue was freaking me out. She continued with more Meryl Streep, chick-flick kind of stuff.

'You really *can't* help it,' she said, her eyes wide with surprise and filled with a newly found inner peace. Hers was an enriched soul, as if descending fresh from a mountain-top pilgrimage, having witnessed the dawning of a new day. I said nothing and continued to blink at her timidly, my eyes the only part of me able to move.

'There, there,' she said gently. 'Now I not only understand but accept what you've been saying to me all these years. It's all become so clear. Every time I bend down and you say, 'While you're down there ...'. Every time I walk past and you squeeze my constantly bruised behind. Every time you wake me in the night with what feels like a broomstick handle in the small of my back. Every time you walk around the bedroom naked expecting that the sight of 'it' will automatically turn me on. Every time you offer to wash my back for me in the shower. Every time you ask me if I have a headache ... you *really can't* help it! It *does* have a mind of its own.'

It was then that she told me how she had just come from the baby's room, how it was a hot day and apart from his nappy junior was naked. She had placed him up on his change table and with both of his hands stretched back behind his head he was doing his best 'Mr February' centrefold pose. He looked at Mum with a strange, impish expression she'd never seen before. As she slowly removed his nappy, expecting to be greeted by the usual mess, who should stand up and introduce himself but the Jolly Jumper himself. Firm, determined and proud, standing rigid to attention she could almost hear it say, 'Howdy ma'am! Pleased to meet you!'

That's right, at the age of less than three months our son had presented his startled mother with his first Raging Roger. I know you'll understand when I tell you I was extremely impressed! My baby son — who had already enriched my life in ways beyond description — now gave me another gift: validity for lecherous male behaviour!

Our baby laughs and giggles and every day with him is a new adventure I can't wait to begin. But possibly, most importantly he's brought me and my wife even closer. Considering I was already deliriously in love with her to begin with, this is something else. Not only do I love her for who she is, but also for now being the mother of my child — and for not just understanding but finally accepting the fact that I, like men everywhere, really can't help it!

Long live the drones!

5-MINUTE TEST-YOURSELF CHECKLIST

So now you've read about just some of the complex, frustrating, secretive and downright weird things that come along with being a father. There's plenty more to know, but sadly there's only so much a book can tell you. Men are experiential learners after all and nothing can take the place of hands-on experience. If you're still not convinced of your suitability for fatherhood, try this quick quiz.

Question 1.

When driving home from the hospital after baby's birth, do you remember to take:

a) The new mum and the flowers?
b) The new mum, the flowers and the cards?
c) The new mum, the flowers, the cards and the gifts?
d) The new mum, the flowers, the cards, the gifts ... and the baby?

Question 2.

The baby cries. Do you:

a) Hand it to its mother?

b) Hand it to its grandmother?

c) Hand it to the first female you see walking past the house at the time?

d) Walk out of the room saying, 'It wasn't me! I didn't do it!'?

Question 3.

The baby doesn't look like you. Do you:

a) Not worry because day-old babies don't look like anyone except day-old babies?

b) Secretly pluck one of baby's hairs and rush to the nearest DNA laboratory?

c) Turn a bright light into the eyes of the baby's mother and demand to know where she was on the night in question nine months earlier?

d) Try to force the baby back where it came from and demand a refund?

Question 4.

Your partner's breasts are:

a) Hers?

b) Yours?

c) The baby's?

d) All of the above?

Question 5.

The baby vomits all over itself and Mum. Do you:

a) Point and laugh?
b) Scream like a big girl and run from the house?
c) Offer to help clean up (knowing Mum will push you away because you'll only add to the mess and confusion)?
d) Reach for a beer, turn on the footy and tell your wife to try to keep the baby quiet?

Question 6.

You haven't had more than thirty minutes unbroken sleep in six months. Your wife or partner is jealous you've had so much more sleep than her. Knowing she's seriously sleep deprived do you:

a) Tell her that's what she gets for being a woman?
b) Tell her she's being neurotic and carefully hide the carving knife?
c) Take the baby out for a drive to let her get some sleep?
d) Try and jump her, knowing she's too weak to fight back?

Question 7.

One month after the birth, baby doesn't seem to do much more than sleep, eat, cry and poop. Do you:

a) Think you may have a dud?
b) Tell people being a dad isn't much fun?
c) Tell people being a dad isn't much fun but you'll give it another week?
d) Join the navy and tell the mother you expect something more interesting to have developed on your return from duty in three years?

HOW TO SCORE

The correct answer to questions 1, 2, 3, 5, 6 and 7 is whichever the mother says is correct. The answer to question 4 is 'B' — you are simply loaning them to your baby.

GLOSSARY

The following are some of the new words and phrases you will, as a dad, be expected to know how to spell, understand and use correctly in a sentence. For a full and comprehensive understanding follow each definition to its conclusion.

announcement: A 'life-as-you-know-it' shattering moment. (See 'epiphany')

attending the birth: Your presence at a 'beautiful moment' full of blood and guts and screaming.

Baby Lands: The greatest investment opportunity since the Indians sold Manhattan. (See 'Pram-tastic')

belittled: (See 'cowed')

birthing suite: Nice word for operating theatre.

blocked ducts: (See 'cracked nipples')

cack: (See 'crap')

cowed: (See 'defeated')

cracked nipple: (See 'mastitis')

crap: (See 'do-do')

crappies: What nappies should be called and something that men have been belittled into learning about. (See 'belittled')

daydreaming: What chicks do when thinking of the future. (See 'visualising')

defeated: (See 'submissive')

design fault: The result of incomplete gestation periods. (See 'soft spot')

do-do: (See 'poo')

domestic blindness: Female term used to denigrate men who suffer a physical and possibly psychological impairment.

domestic duties: (See 'women's work')

dreaming: The time when fathers have sex. (See 'sex')

drone: Unnecessary life form required for no other reason except the provision of sperm. (See 'sperm')

enlightened: A trick and a lie to make men deal with what should be exclusively a woman's domain. (See 'domestic duties')

epiphany: 1. The manifestation of a supernatural or divine reality. 2. Any moment of great or sudden revelation. Latin from the Greek *epiphaneia*, 'an appearing', plus *phainein*, 'to show'. (See 'announcement')

episiotomy: Look it up for yourself pal, I'm not going there! (See 'blocked ducts')

father: (See 'drone')

fontanelle: (See 'design fault')

hangover: Affliction regularly visited upon men for the simple sin of trying to enjoy themselves. (See 'morning sickness')

hormones: Why do you want to know?! What would you want to ask for *at a time like this you selfish, insensitive pig?! I hate you!*

mastitis: (See 'episiotomy')

morning sickness: (See 'hangover')

mucus: (See 'poo')

night time: The time of day other people sleep. (See 'Others')

others: (See 'pre-parents')

parent: Despite just about everything in this book, the best thing in the world you could ever wish to be.

perspective: What you need to adjust in order to survive these enlightened times. (See 'enlightened')

playpen: Nice word for 'cage'.

poo: Bodily waste dealt with exclusively by women until more enlightened times. (See 'enlightened')

pram: Expensive billy cart you're not allowed to race.

Pramtastic: Subsidiary of Baby Lands. (See 'Baby Lands')

pre-parents: Potential parents.

sex: What got you into this predicament. (See 'dreaming')

sleep: The twenty minutes a day between feeding, changing, burping, bathing, feeding, changing, tidying, feeding, changing, feeding and burping the baby. (See 'dreaming')

smock: Pregnant version of the little black dress.

soft spot: (See 'fontanelle')

sperm: The reason women allow us to exist.
(See 'father')

submissive: The state modern-day fathers have been reduced to. (See 'belittled')

suckle: Nice word for 'feeding'. (See 'cracked nipples')

support: Who knows? Could be anything. Ask your woman, it's up to her.

useless know nothing: (See 'father')

visualising: What men do when they are focused on achieving success in the future. (See 'daydreaming')

vomit: (See 'poo')

women: The *fairer* sex. Can't live with them, can't live with them!

women's work: (See 'perspective')